Pueblo Bonito and Chaco Canyon Revisited

FIGURE 1. Newspaper obituary photograph of George Hubbard Pepper, taken ca. 1918.

FIGURE 2. Ca. 1900 photograph of Richard Wetherill. Photographer unidentified.

Pueblo Bonito AND *Chaco Canyon* REVISITED

The Published versus the Unpublished Record

Jonathan E. Reyman

UNIVERSITY OF NEW MEXICO PRESS   ALBUQUERQUE

© 2024 by the University of New Mexico Press

All rights reserved. Published 2024

Printed in the United States of America

ISBN 978-0-8263-6650-4 (cloth)
ISBN 978-0-8263-6651-1 (paper)
ISBN 978-0-8263-6652-8 (ePub)
ISBN 978-0-8263-6741-9 (webPDF)

Library of Congress Cataloging-in-Publication data is on file with the Library of Congress.

Founded in 1889, the University of New Mexico sits on the traditional homelands of the Pueblo of Sandia. The original peoples of New Mexico—Pueblo, Navajo, and Apache—since time immemorial have deep connections to the land and have made significant contributions to the broader community statewide. We honor the land itself and those who remain stewards of this land throughout the generations and also acknowledge our committed relationship to Indigenous peoples. We gratefully recognize our history.

Cover illustration: James Bingham (1917–1971), *Pueblo Bonito, Chaco Canyon ca. 1067*. 1968 Celotex Corporation print (author's collection).

Designed by Isaac Morris

Composed in Scala Pro

For Laura, as always

CONTENTS

ix	*List of Illustrations*
xi	*List of Tables*
xiii	*Preface*
xv	*Acknowledgments*
1	*Chapter One.* Introduction to the Research on the Burials
10	*Chapter Two.* Chaco Canyon
35	*Chapter Three.* Pueblo Bonito and Chaco Canyon: The Unpublished Record
92	*Chapter Four.* Burial Mounds and Cemeteries
110	*Chapter Five.* Summary and Conclusions
117	*Appendix A.* Images of Skeletal Materials from Pueblo Bonito and the Pepper–Wetherill Mound 5, WSW of Pueblo del Arroyo
127	*Appendix B.* Osteometric Data and Analysis of the Skeletal Materials in Pueblo Bonito Rooms 32–33
	MARTIN K. NICKELS, EDITED BY JONATHAN E. REYMAN
143	*Appendix C.* The Identification and Significance of a Milkweed Seed
147	*Appendix D.* Research Resources
149	*Notes*
157	*References*
169	*Index*

ILLUSTRATIONS

FIGURES

ii	*Figure 1.* George Hubbard Pepper (ca. 1918)
ii	*Figure 2.* Richard Wetherill (ca. 1900)
17	*Figure 3.* Phoebe Apperson Hearst
18	*Figure 4.* Santa Clara Pueblo pottery collected by Pepper for Phoebe Apperson Hearst
19	*Figure 5.* First Wetherill trading post and general store (1895–1896)
19	*Figure 6.* Second Wetherill trading post and permanent home (1896)
51	*Figure 7.* The large burial site Mound 5
56	*Figure 8.* Pepper's 1896 stratigraphic profile for Room 32, Pueblo Bonito
57–61	*Figures 9–15.* Pepper's 1896 field drawings of the skeletal materials in Rooms 32–33, Pueblo Bonito
77–79	*Figures 16–18.* Drawings of the burial and contents in Pueblo Bonito Rooms 32–33
103	*Figure 19.* Casa Rinconada and two small burial mounds
118	*Figure A.1.* Slab-lined or cist grave in Mound 5
118	*Figure A.2.* Windblown debris atop burial mound at Chaco Canyon
122–125	*Figures A.3–A.8.* Burials from Mound 5
144	*Figure C.1.* Stevenson drawing of a milkweed seed

PLATES

15	*Plate 1.* Aerial photograph of wall between Pueblo Bonito and Chetro Ketl
71	*Plate 2.* Turquoise-inlaid shell bird
87	*Plate 3.* Pseudo-cloisonné invested basalt mortar
95–97	*Plates 4–5.* Richard and Marietta Wetherill's gravesite
113–115	*Plates 6–7.* Painted "altar cloth"
119	*Plate A.1.* Cranium H/3671 (skeleton 13) showing cut mark on the lower left parietal bone
120–121	*Plates A.2–A.4.* Cranium H/3672 (skeleton 14) showing puncture wounds and other major damage

TABLES

138	*Table B.1.* Individual skull measurements
139	*Table B.2.* Pubic symphyseal age assessments
140	*Table B.3.* Comparative non-metric traits frequencies
141	*Table B.4.* Comparative cranial facial metrics

PREFACE

This study began in 1968 with my first visit to Chaco Canyon and continued for almost fifty-five years, first as part of the research for my doctoral dissertation (Reyman 1971) and then in an ongoing effort to discover the rest of the story about Chaco burials. Some aspects of this work were published or otherwise reported over the years (Nickels and Reyman 1981; Reyman 1978a, 1982, 1985, 1989, 1995a and b; Reyman and Nickels 1981), but for reasons discussed later, the completion of the research was delayed and this report could not be published until now, more than a century after George H. Pepper, Richard Wetherill, their Navajo workers, Warren K. Moorehead, and others first uncovered these materials in the rooms of Pueblo Bonito and in other sites within the confines of Chaco Canyon.

Much of the excavated materials, archaeological field notes, and photographs are extant, although, as discussed more fully in the pages that follow, some crucial materials are missing and apparently unrecoverable. This is a frustrating and oftentimes almost maddening situation, as the reader will learn. Nevertheless, given the content and context of these existing materials and their importance for Chacoan archaeology, the time is long overdue to publish as complete a report as possible, including a brief history of Pepper's original excavation of the so-called burial rooms at Pueblo Bonito and his analysis of their contents. Related materials from other rooms at Pueblo Bonito and sites at Chaco Canyon excavated by Pepper and Wetherill are also considered, as are the investigative survey of S. J. Holsinger (1901), the excavations of Moorehead (1906), Edgar Hewett's fieldwork (1921, 1936), Neil Judd's excavations (1930, 1954, 1959, 1964), and some of the later work by the Chacoan field schools (e.g., Brand et al. 1937, Kluckhohn and Reiter 1939). Finally, published reports by still later archaeologists from the Chaco Center and other institutions are discussed to indicate the range and diversity of scholarly interest in Chacoan archaeology in the last several decades as well as provide Chacoan scholars with useful comparative data on and an overview of Ancestral Puebloan burial practices at Chaco Canyon (e.g., Akins 1986, 2003; Akins and Schelberg 1984; Crown 2016, 2020; Crown and Hurst 2009; Crown, Marden, and Mattson 2016; Kennett et al. 2017; Lekson 1984b, 1988; Marden 2011; Mills 2018; Mills and Ferguson 2008; Plog and Heitman 2006, 2010; Windes 1984). Finally, and importantly, this report is intended to demonstrate the value of unpublished records—original notes, photographs, and other documents housed in museums, libraries, and archives—materials that have been overlooked, forgotten, discounted, or ignored, but that contain primary data essential to our understanding of the past and the history of our profession.

ACKNOWLEDGMENTS

This report could not have been written, and certainly not completed, without the help of a great many individuals, and it is important to start at the beginning. Walter W. Taylor, J. Charles Kelley, Charles H. Lange, and Carroll L. Riley provided guidance, encouragement, and direct assistance via university support for the initial research. All have now departed and are sorely missed. Richard A. Gould and Paul Malot of the American Museum of Natural History and other AMNH staff members, especially Anibal Rodriguez, Jr., Barbara Conklin, Priscilla Ward, Gordon F. Ekholm, David Hurst Thomas, Harry Shapiro, Harold Feinberg, and N. Norma Feinberg provided access to the Pepper Collection at the museum and research assistance. Anibal Rodriguez, Jr. also provided photographs of important materials.

Brenda Shears Holland and Nancy A. Henry of the (then) Museum of the American Indian, Heye Foundation were similarly helpful with our work on the Pepper Collection and Wetherill's field notes at that museum and in its separate Bronx, New York, repository. Donald J. Werner and Natasha Bonilla helped me photograph some of the artifacts and Brenda Shears Holland later provided additional photographs of objects that we identified at the museum's storage facility in the Bronx.

We received wonderful cooperation and assistance from the Anthropology Department staff at the Smithsonian Institution, especially Douglas H. Ubelaker, T. Dale Stewart, Donald J. Ortner, Joseph Brown, Clara Ann Simmons, and Robert Elder during our work with Neil M. Judd's Chacoan collections from Pueblo Bonito and Pueblo del Arroyo. Harry and Marion Slatin provided housing while we worked at the Smithsonian.

At Tulane University, former director Thomas Niehaus, Ruth R. Olivera, Mary Bass-Halford, and Martin Sweaney of the Latin American Library and E. Wyllys Andrews V, former director of the Middle American Research Institute, and his assistant, Kathe Lawton, were most generous in permitting full access to the Pepper collections, and Andrews and Lawton arranged for Harriett Blum to duplicate important photographs and lantern slides.

Charles H. Lange, Dorothy Keur, Donald Brand, and Jeanette Pepper Cameron (George Pepper's daughter) and her husband, James Cameron, all helped to locate formerly missing portions of Pepper's notes and other materials, and the Camerons provided critical information about Pepper. Thomas E. Holien provided invaluable technical information on painted and invested ceramics and other archaeological objects.

Richard Hardin and Walter Herriman, former superintendents at Chaco Canyon National Monument (now Chaco Culture National Historical Park), were most cooperative during my fieldwork there. W. James Judge, Dwight Drager, and James Ebert provided access to Chaco Center archaeological records and remote sensing data for Chaco Canyon, and Drager and Ebert instructed me on the interpretation of aerial photographs. Karli White transferred the WordStar copy of Pepper and Wetherill's unpublished materials into Word format.

Gloria J. Fenner, Susan R. Harris, and Kathe Klobnak of the National Park Service, Western Archaeological Research Center, provided photographs and data on Pueblo Bonito burials. J. Jefferson Reid's "cattle prod" comments forced me to refine some of my arguments.

C. K. Brain of the Transvaal Museum in South Africa aided in the ultimately unsuccessful search for skeletal material from the Pepper collections sent to Robert Broom in 1914 by Aleš Hrdlička of the American Museum of Natural History. James Baldoni developed and printed some of the black-and-white photographs used in this volume. Steven LeBlanc of the Peabody Museum provided provenience data for several skeletal remains at that museum.

Julianne Snider, then with the Illinois State Museum, created the fine drawings of the never-before-illustrated Pueblo Bonito burial tomb complex in Rooms 32–33, which truly enhance this volume.

The late C. Randall Morrison, a true Socratic gadfly and a dear friend for more than fifty years, was a constant source of irritation, stimulation, and encouragement, and this report is a result, in significant measure, of his trenchant comments and persistent urging to get on with the research.

Research support was provided by National Science Foundation grants GS-2829 and BNS8701657, Wenner-Gren Foundation Grant-in-Aid 4012, an Andrew W. Mellon Foundation grant, grants from Southern Illinois University, and summer research grants from Illinois State University. The late Mrs. Lita Osmundsen, then Director of Research for Wenner-Gren, was most helpful making financial arrangements in New York City for the 1980 summer research.

Doug Carr, former Illinois State Museum staff photographer, colleague, and good friend, provided needed technical assistance: he cleaned the 125-year-old Pepper–Wetherill photographs and lantern slides, inked Pepper's field drawings done in now-faded pencil, and worked to upgrade the appearance of all visuals, as well as my three commissioned drawings, and then transferred everything to a digital format for publication.

Stephen Lekson, F. Joan Mathien, Stephen Plog, Jill Neitzel, R. Gwinn Vivian, and Joe Watkins read and commented on earlier drafts of manuscripts from which material has been drawn for this volume. Lekson's, Mathien's, and Watkins' comments and suggestions were especially helpful, and I am deeply grateful to all three of them for their time and efforts. The authors alone are responsible for errors of fact or interpretation.

Katherine Harper did superb work in editing the manuscript, such that, at times, she seemed to know what I wanted to say better than I knew myself. Thanks also to Michael Goldstein for compiling the index.

Finally, my thanks and appreciation go to Michael Millman, senior acquisitions editor at the University of New Mexico Press, for his invaluable assistance in guiding the manuscript through the long process to publication.

CHAPTER ONE

Introduction to the Research on the Burials

AS NOTED IN THE preface, this research project began more than fifty-five years ago, in 1968, as one component, though not a major one at the time, of my dissertation research (Reyman 1971) on Mesoamerican–Southwestern interaction. I specifically wanted to examine what I thought were likely Mesoamerican or Mesoamerican-influenced materials from Pueblo Bonito and other sites at Chaco Canyon excavated by the Hyde Exploring Expedition (1896–1901), which were housed at the American Museum of Natural History and the Museum of the American Indian, Heye Foundation. Toward that end, I secured a National Science Foundation doctoral dissertation grant and permission from the American Museum and other institutions for collections research. Dr. Richard Gould was my liaison at the American Museum of Natural History, and he assigned Paul Malot of the Department of Anthropology to collaborate with me. Dr. Frederick Dockstader, then director of the Museum of the American Indian, was my original contact person at that institution but provided help from the various staff members noted above.

The initial collections research at the two institutions was conducted in the winter of 1970–1971. The conditions at the American Museum were less than ideal. Many of Pepper's and Wetherill's artifact collections there, especially the turquoise, the ceramics, and the more exotic objects (with some notable exceptions) were in the Southwest Hall. The hall had been closed years before. There was no electricity, and I was not permitted to take the objects to a better-lit room. The examination had to be conducted using the dim winter light that filtered through two filthy windows, and the photography was done by the same light plus my camera flash.

CHAPTER ONE

Several of the exotic objects, such as the so-called painted altar cloth from Room 13 (Pepper 1920, 68–69) and the painted flutes from Rooms 25 (Pepper 1920, 109) and 33 (Pepper 1909, 199–205; Pepper 1920, 164–66) were stored in a large collections range along with the Pueblo Bonito and miscellaneous Chacoan objects not on display. More of the Hyde Exploring Expedition collection was on exhibit or stored at the Museum of the American Indian, Heye Foundation. The same was true for the Pepper and Wetherill field notes, photographs, and other documents; most were stored in an attic at the American Museum, reachable via a pull-down ladder, and the rest, or so I thought at the time, were in the library and attic at the Museum of the American Indian and its warehouse in the Bronx. I was able to complete the research necessary for the component of my dissertation that was based on these collections, but it became clear during the work that there was a wealth of unpublished material which required examination and analyses, and I would have to return to New York City at a later date. This eventually became a decades-long odyssey that took me to some twenty-two institutions across the United States, some visited several times, such as the Middle American Research Institute at Tulane University, the Maxwell Museum, and the former Chaco Center, and to meet with, write, or telephone dozens of individuals who had known Pepper, Wetherill, and others involved with the early work at Chaco Canyon, most notably Pepper's daughter, Jeanette Cameron, her husband, James, and her professor and mentor at the University of New Mexico, Dorothy Keur.

Eventually the question arose as to whether the burials in Rooms 32–33 at Pueblo Bonito, especially the two beneath the prepared wooden plank floor in Room 33, might be those of Mesoamerican individuals (Reyman 1978a). Pepper (1909) had described and discussed the condition of the twelve skeletons in the fill above the floor, noting that the skulls and mandibles were often disarticulated from the postcranial remains. I wanted to examine the skeletal remains to determine whether any of the individuals had been decapitated, as might be expected of sacrificial victims. Although I had done skeletal analyses as part of my graduate training, I did not feel competent to conduct the examinations, so I asked my Illinois State University colleague Martin K. Nickels to accompany me to the American Museum. We obtained permission from the Department of Anthropology at the Museum to do the work, and we also asked and obtained permission from T. Dale Stewart, who had earlier (1935) worked with the materials and later published a brief report (Stewart 1975). In a letter to me (Stewart 1979b), Stewart graciously wrote, "After all this time I have lost any publishing priority I may have had. So feel free to go ahead with whatever you are planning along this line."

Supported by a Wenner-Gren Foundation grant and funds from Illinois State University, Nickels and I arrived at the museum in late June 1980. Since I had first worked at the AMNH in winter 1970–1971, the materials had been moved from the Southwest Hall to storage, and the collections had been rearranged and catalogued to make research easier. Curatorial assistant Anibal Rodriguez was assigned to help us and had taken out the boxes containing the skeletal materials for our examination and study, as well as the turquoise, shell, and pseudo-cloisonné items (ceramic, wood, and basketry), copper bells, flutes, and most of the other exotic objects, notably the jet frog and inlay work from Room 38 (Pepper 1920, 184–95), in some cases for restudy from my 1970–1971 work. The cylinder jars from Room 28 and elsewhere in Pueblo Bonito were made available, and we also looked through the collection range cabinets, drawer by drawer, for further objects of interest. The "painted altar cloth" had been removed from its crate and was much more accessible for our examination than a decade earlier. There were even x-ray images to consult.

We received an immediate surprise when we began work on the skeletal materials. Nancy Akins notes (1986, ix) that she visited the American Museum in 1979 to measure and examine the skeletal materials, specifically to make cranial measurements.[1] Nickels and I visited the AMNH in spring and summer of 1980. Yet when we opened the boxes of Rooms 32–33 skeletal materials to begin our examination, the crania and most of the postcranial bones were covered with a thick black dust, possibly asbestos, that *seemed* to have accumulated over years. The only logical explanation seemed to be that it had reaccumulated in the attics between Akins's visit and ours. Regardless, it was necessary to don masks, goggles, and gloves and brush and vacuum the bones before studying them. Kerriann Marden (2011) did not mention any dust in her study conducted about thirty years later, so it's certainly possible that the skeletal materials she studied were reboxed and stored elsewhere than in the attic. As she states in a footnote:

> In 1980, Martin Nickels and Jonathan Reyman appear to have attempted to sort comingled remains in the AMNH collection. It is unclear whether these researchers were working together or separately, but since the dates on the notes they left at the museum are so closely clustered and their efforts were so similar, it seems most likely that they were working jointly. However, these researchers' efforts seem to have stopped after trying to sort the long bones into pairs or sets. Reyman left a few typed note cards in the boxes with the remains, whereas Nickels' cards have been separated out and placed in the accession file. Neither appears to have ever published his results from this attempt (Marden 2011, 193).

It would not have taken Marden much effort to contact us to learn that we did work together, what our results were, and where they were available: for example, we gave papers at a Society for American Archaeology meeting, and I published some results.

Another curious fact became known to us shortly thereafter. Pepper (1909) reported finding the skeletal remains of fourteen individuals in Room 33. There were fourteen postcranial skeletons but only thirteen crania: H/3667, presumably Pepper's skull number 9 (Pepper 1909, 219), had been "exchanged" with Dr. Robert Broom in South Africa in 1914 by Aleš Hrdlička, a not-uncommon practice in the early twentieth century. We contacted Dr. C. K. Brain of the Transvaal Museum in an attempt to locate the skull and to obtain measurements, but he was unable to find it at the Museum (it was originally labeled H/3667 in ink), nor could he discover what had happened to it.

The results of Nickels' examination and analyses of the skeletal remains are published in Appendix B to this volume. We found no evidence that any individuals in the fill of Room 33 had been decapitated, but individuals 13 and 14 beneath the prepared wooden floor had suffered perimortem trauma. However, they were not significantly different physically from other Chacoan and Southwest populations. Thus our hypotheses that they were Mesoamericans was not confirmed. Nevertheless, it was clear that individual 13 probably had been murdered and that individual 14 certainly was. The photographs in the text and in Appendices A and

B make it clear that this was no "accident," as Pepper suggested (1909, 249) but that "Both exhibited chopping and percussion blows to the head, suggesting violent deaths" (Akins and Schelberg 1984, 91). The three crania that Moorehead (1906) excavated from Pueblo Bonito (57024A, 57033A, and 57049A) and stored at Harvard's Peabody Museum also met violent ends, as indicated by the large perimortem puncture wounds in their crania.

Some objects found in Rooms 32–33 (and also in Room 28 and elsewhere), however, are clearly of Mesoamerican origin, such as the conch shell trumpets. Others are of Mesoamerican derivation or association, such as the cylindrical ceramic jars that have been shown to hold remnants of cacao (Crown and Hurst 2009). Pepper (1920, 121) thought they might well have been Mesoamerican in origin, specifically from the Cakchiquel Maya.

Following the work at the American Museum, Nickels and I moved our research uptown to the Museum of the American Indian, Heye Foundation. There was a wealth of material there as well, more than we could examine in the time we had, and I decided to return the following summer (1981). We then went to Washington, DC to work on Neil M. Judd's materials from Pueblo Bonito housed at the Smithsonian, specifically the pseudo-cloisonné, copper bells, inlay work, and other objects likely of Mesoamerican derivation or influence.

The summer 1981 research at the Museum of the American Indian yielded Wetherill's field notes, most importantly those on the Pepper–Wetherill excavations in Chacoan burial mounds and cemeteries, plus photographs, some of which I had copied. I had not expected to find these things; indeed, I did not know that Wetherill had taken notes on the work. So when I discovered within the Hyde Exploring Expedition/Pueblo Bonito file in the library of the Museum of the American Indian a packet of treated brown paper tied with string, I could not imagine what it contained. It held Wetherill's field notes, almost perfectly preserved (if a bit yellowed with age), including notes on burial mounds.

I next went to the Southwest Cultural Resources Center at the University of New Mexico in 1982 to examine aerial photographs to see whether the burial mounds and cemeteries and other features mentioned in the Pepper and Wetherill notes were still visible and to look at the photographs that Jeanette Cameron had given to Dorothy Keur who, in turn, had donated them to the Anthropology Department at UNM in the mid-to-late 1930s.

I made several trips to the Middle American Research Institute and the Latin American Library at Tulane University (1984–1989) to study their Pepper materials, sold to the MARI by Jessie Crellin Pepper, Pepper's widow, after his death in 1924. Summer in New Orleans is unpleasant: hot, humid, buggy, with frequent pop-up thunderstorms. I welcomed the repositories' air conditioning and ceiling fans. I found more information on Chaco burials, burial mounds (including photographs of some of the burials in the large Mound 5 across the Chaco arroyo west-southwest of Pueblo del Arroyo), more of Pepper's Chacoan field notes, his field diaries, ethnographic notes, and collections, lantern slides (including hand-colored ones), some of which I had copied, and other materials.

My research was focused on the Hyde Exploring Expedition's 1896–1901 archaeological fieldwork at Chaco Canyon. To some scholars, including me, Chaco Canyon was (and still is) an other-worldly place of ruins large and small, mesas, the spectacular Fajada Butte, brilliant sunlight, a night sky filled with countless stars made clearer by the absence of ambient light (at least in the 1970s and 1980s), and violent thunderstorms with flash floods, all set amid a high Sonoran plateau with mostly scrub vegetation. Chaco has distinctive odors: the sandstone used to build the ancient architecture; alkali, the soil, and dust after rainfall; sage, mesquite, tamarisk, ephedra, and other plants; ozone after thunder and lightning; and a host of others. If I closed my eyes, I'd know I was in Chaco Canyon just from the distinctive scents I experienced.

The Reading Room at the Latin American Library was also a special place, with its dark wood paneling, the tables with their green-shaded brass reading lamps, the leather armchairs, the high ceiling, the windows that allowed in the outside light, and the silence interrupted only by the sound of turning pages. There were strict rules for using the room, some established because of peculiar problems that beset libraries, such as the theft of rare books and also criminal vandalism—marking books and cutting out pages. Because of these problems, the library established fixed strictures and handed out a list of them to visitors:

INTRODUCTION TO THE RESEARCH ON THE BURIALS

- No overcoats, outer jackets, backpacks, brief cases, bags, and large purses;
- No pens or markers; only lead pencils, mechanical or sharpened [A sharpener was in the room];
- No food or drinks;
- Only note pads and index cards permitted [this was before laptop computers];
- Rulers and magnifying glasses are permitted;
- Librarians bring the requested books, maps, and other materials to you which must be signed for when received and signed out when one is finished with them;
- No loud conversations and no music;
- and cotton gloves are provided and must be worn when handling rare or damaged materials.

Each morning I arrived shortly after 8:00 with my list of items to read and my briefcase filled with pads, index cards, mechanical pencils, ruler, and magnifying glass. I removed everything from my briefcase other than what was permitted and stored it in a locker. I entered the Reading Room, handed my list to the librarian, walked to my table with my back to a high window, and waited for the books and other materials to arrive. My work day began.

The Latin American Library Reading Room was not just a place of research: for me, it was also the location of one of my strangest experiences regarding Chaco Canyon. It was a veritable time machine but without dials and electronic components. I was stunned the first time I seemingly was transported back to the past—to late nineteenth-century Chaco Canyon. This occurred every day, to the point that I couldn't wait to begin work each morning.

As I started reading, it was as if a veil dropped between me and the room and I was in Chaco Canyon. Depending on what I was reading, I could smell the sandstone, the dust, nearby plants, the ozone after a severe storm. Beyond this, I heard the creak of wagons, the snorts of horses and mules, and general human voices, although not specific words. I saw George Pepper, Richard Wetherill and his brother-in-law, Orion Buck,

CHAPTER ONE

Richard's wife Marietta, and the Navajo fieldworkers. This happened every day for the rest of my time in the library reading room and in subsequent summers there as well.

At the end of each day, when the librarian came to say the library was closing, the spell—the reverie—broke. I had not gotten up from my seat for the eight hours. I had not taken a break for lunch or used the men's room. For almost a month, this was my daily routine. I never left my chair because I was in Chaco Canyon with the 1896–1901 Hyde Exploring Expedition. I saw the canyon and its ruins, smelled the place, heard the sounds. It was the closest I ever came to time travel. Magic was in the Reading Room—something I've never experienced at any other place. And when I returned later to Chaco for more fieldwork, it was with an almost oppressive sense of déjà vu.

My MARI and Latin American Library work led, in turn, to collections research at other institutions, including the Field Museum of Natural History (1988), then back to Tulane (1989), then to several institutions in New Mexico and Arizona. I even spent half a day fruitlessly searching in the small town of Thoreau, New Mexico, from which the Hyde Exploring Expedition rail-shipped the Chaco materials to New York City. Finally I traveled to the Peabody Museum at Harvard with Nickels (1990) to look at skeletal materials and artifacts from Moorehead's April 1897 work at Pueblo Bonito and Chaco Canyon (Moorehead 1906) and W. C. Farabee's 1901 Peabody Museum expedition to Chaco and elsewhere in the Southwest. I knew that Moorehead had been associated with the Robert S. Peabody Institute of Archaeology at Phillips Academy at Andover, Massachusetts at the time he worked at Chaco Canyon. However, the vast majority of his collections there were from the Eastern Woodlands, and there was nothing useful of his for Chaco Canyon.

Interspersed among my work from the early 1970s onward were interviews and correspondence with a number of individuals who had direct or indirect connections to Pepper, such as Jeanette Cameron and her husband, Pepper's son-in-law, James Cameron (though he never met Pepper), Dorothy Keur, and Homer Hastings. Finally, between 1968 and the mid-1980s, I conducted fieldwork almost every year at Chaco Canyon and was able to check some of Pepper and Wetherill's reported findings in the canyon and its environs (e.g., Reyman 1989, 49). I received some long sought-after data on several Chaco burials in January 2010. Although I am certain there are more unpublished data waiting to be discovered and analyzed, the time is past due to close this effort on Pepper and Wetherill's work and to publish the results.

CHAPTER TWO

Chaco Canyon

CHACO CANYON, NEW MEXICO has been of historical interest to scholars for almost two hundred years. The first written description was apparently made in 1823 by Colonel José Antonio Vizcarra, who called it the Arroyo de San Carlos:

> According to indications the water is not permanent, but on this march it has been found always flowing. There are good fields for the pasturing of stock and superior lands for planting by dry farming . . . the ruins of several pueblos were found, which were of such antiquity that their inhabitants were not known to Europeans (qtd. in Brugge 1964, 227).

Archaeological reconnaissance began with Lieutenant James H. Simpson's 1849 exploration of the canyon (Simpson 1850). Simpson and his assistants, notably the brothers Edward and Richard Kern, mapped the area and sketched many of the major ruins that today are variously referred to as "great pueblos," "great houses," or town sites. A quarter-century later, in 1875, Oscar Loew briefly surveyed Chaco Canyon, followed in 1877 by photographer William Henry Jackson, a member of the US Geological and Geographical Survey of the Territories led by F. V. Hayden. Still later, others found their way to the site, including Victor Mindeleff, who, in 1888, surveyed and photographed the major archaeological ruins for the Bureau of American Ethnology (Mindeleff 1891), then under the direction of Major J. W. Powell.

The Hyde Exploring Expedition (1896–1901) conducted the first large-scale archaeological excavations at Chaco Canyon. Frederick Ward Putnam was director of the project but was largely absent, leaving his young protégé, George H. Pepper, in charge of the day-to-day operations, assisted by Richard Wetherill, several of Wetherill's relatives, and a crew of Navajo men. Although Pepper and his crew excavated at several sites throughout the canyon and its environs, the main focus of the expedition was Pueblo Bonito (Pepper 1909, 1920).

Twenty years later, the National Geographic Society sponsored another major multiyear excavation (1921–1927) at Pueblo Bonito (Judd 1954, 1964) and at nearby Pueblo del Arroyo (Judd 1959). It was during this period and for a few years afterward that astronomer A. E. Douglass collected tree-ring samples from these and other Chacoan sites, research that eventually resulted in the development of dendrochronology in the American Southwest (Douglass 1935). The abovementioned fieldwork and subsequent archaeological research are discussed at length by various scholars, e.g., Hewett (1936a), Lister and Lister (1981), Reyman (1989), Elliott (1995), and Snead (2001).

Given the overall time involved (more than a century) and the enormous amount of archaeological research done at Chaco Canyon and at Pueblo Bonito, the largest (in terms of the number of rooms) and best-known Chacoan site, it is probably not surprising that much of the archaeological data and analyses remain unpublished. Pepper, for example, had only brief statements to make about Rooms 116–190 at Pueblo Bonito:

> Minor excavations were made in a number of rooms ranging from 116 to 190. Nothing of special interest was developed in these excavations aside from the specimens shown in Figures 138 to 154 (Pepper 1920, 339).

In fact, not only were some interesting artifacts recovered from Rooms 116–190—among them a jet object with a "Bird Wing Design" (Pepper 1920, figure 138), a painted wooden object, perhaps a flower from an altar (figure 139), and a frog effigy vessel (figure 142)—but Room 190 was an unusual circular structure with a paved stone floor. Furthermore, figure 154 pictures a burial and grave goods with skeleton 20, which was excavated in Mound 2 and *not* in Pueblo Bonito.

Many of the so-called Bc or Hosta Butte Phase sites were excavated in whole or in part as archaeological field school projects sponsored by the University of New Mexico, the School of American Research, Harvard University, and other institutions. This was the case at Bc-47, Bc-53, Bc-56, Bc-57, Bc-58, and Bc-59, among other Hosta Butte Phase sites. Most results were never published.

Bc-26 served as the basis for Bertha Dutton's 1937 MA thesis, which was published the following year (Dutton 1938). However, the results of the archaeological fieldwork at the two most famous Bc sites, Bc-50 and Bc-51, were published only as incomplete, preliminary reports (Brand et al. 1937; Kluckhohn and Reiter 1939).

Several major sites such as Chetro Ketl, Talus Unit No. 1 (directly behind Chetro Ketl), and Kin Nahasbas were also first excavated as field school projects. Some of these results were published (e.g., Hawley 1934; Hewett 1936), and much later a stabilization project was documented at Kin Nahasbas (Mathien and Windes 1987). Despite the 1930s work being relatively well known (e.g., Luhrs 1935; Miller 1937; Woods 1935), most of the reports have never appeared in print.

Other major sources of unpublished data are the Ruins Stabilization Reports for most of the Chacoan great houses and town sites, and also for some smaller sites. These reports describe the repair and stabilization work done at the sites since at least the 1940s, with "before and after" photographs to illustrate the work. They are invaluable for this information alone because they improve our understanding of the archaeological history of the sites as they now exist, versus their appearance in previous years and decades (see, e.g., Reyman 1978b). The changes are often significant.

The Ruin Stabilization Reports also include primary data on materials discovered at the sites during the course of the stabilization process, data that are not published or available elsewhere. For example, while I was working at Pueblo Bonito in the summer of 1974, a crew also working at the site dismantled a masonry wall to repair and stabilize it and found a small ceramic bowl and stick (*paho?*) that apparently had been placed in the wall as offerings at the time of construction some nine hundred to one thousand years earlier. To the best of my knowledge, the description of these objects and the context of their discovery appear only in the stabilization report for that summer's work at Pueblo Bonito.

A much more significant example of this same type of situation occurred at Chetro Ketl in August 1947 when an unusually heavy rainstorm—a "frog choker" in Southwest parlance—caused the partial collapse of the back wall of the pueblo. During the course of the repair and stabilization process, the National Park Service Ruins Stabilization Unit excavated Room 93. The room contained more than two hundred wooden ritual objects, some of which were originally part of one or more ceremonial altars. For various reasons (see Vivian et al. 1978, 1–3), this important assemblage remained undescribed in the literature for over thirty years.

Contrary to the old adage, it is often the case in archaeology that ignorance is not bliss. Indeed, ignorance, especially of the unpublished record, can lead to wasted fieldwork, serious errors of interpretation, and incorrect conclusions. I have described just such a situation with regard to my own fieldwork at Wupatki (Reyman 1978b), where the relevant Ruins Stabilization Report beforehand was out on loan and my inability to read it led to the erroneous interpretation that a window in Room 44 had been constructed to incorporate astronomical alignments to the winter and summer solstice and the equinox sunrises. Fortunately, the error was pointed out to me *before* publication of the erroneous findings. Such is not always the case. For instance, in 1901 S. J. Holsinger wrote an unpublished but well-known report documenting work at Casa Rinconada in Chaco Canyon. Both photograph 35 in Holsinger's report and an unpublished Hyde Exploring Expedition photograph of the site taken in 1896, probably by Richard Wetherill, show a gaping hole in the wall where the northeast window now exists as a "reconstructed" architectural feature. The latter photograph also shows the presence of a wall *exterior* to the wall in which the northeast window is now situated. This would have blocked the passage of sunlight into the room (Reyman 1982, 907). The exterior wall and room block are also evident in Edgar Hewett's article "The Chaco Canyon and Its Ancient Monuments" (1921, 23). However, in the early 1980s another researcher, unaware of all this earlier scholarship, concluded that the northeast window and Niche E at Casa Rinconada were aligned to the summer solstice sunrise. By the time he learned of his mistake, his assertions were in print (Williamson 1981, 72 and figure 8.7).

Unpublished field notes and diaries are other important sources of primary data. Such notes exist for many sites at Chaco Canyon, both great houses and small pueblos. For example, more recent work at Pueblo Alto concludes that most of the excavated rooms were one story high (Windes and Toll 1987, 342, passim). Perhaps they were, but it must be noted that Richard Wetherill removed a considerable number of timbers and "many wagonloads" of stone from Pueblo Alto to build his nearby mesa-top trading post and later Navajo structures (Wetherill 1896), a situation not unlike one reported by Mrs. Wetherill, as recorded by Gordon Vivian (1948, 3):

> She brought up the story of the wall between Bonito and Chettro Kettle. According to her it was about 4 feet high and extended all the way between the two pueblos. When I asked what became of it she said Dick wouldn't let the Navajo use stone from the ruin so when they built some of the post and residence the Navajo went out and hauled in this wall and it's now in the buildings.

As I wrote earlier (Reyman 1989, 49), archaeologists with whom I spoke about her comment gave little credence to the existence of such a wall, and those who did assumed it extended south from the canyon wall between and generally parallel to the east wall of Pueblo Bonito and the west wall of Chetro Ketl. I read Marietta Wetherill's comments literally—that it "extended all the way between the two pueblos." When I consulted aerial photographs at the Chaco Center and later briefly checked the area between the sites with Randy Morrison, it seemed clear that she was correct. The wall is visible in plate 1 as well as on the ground with a little "scuffing" of the soil.

Again, there is a vast amount of unpublished information for Chaco Canyon that, if made generally available, would markedly change our perceptions and understanding of the archaeological history of Chaco and the cultural history of its ancient Puebloan populations. Many, perhaps most, of these unpublished records are *not* in obscure locations but in the very institutions where one would expect to find them if one knows the history of Chacoan archaeology, e.g., the Smithsonian Institution, National Anthropological Archives, American Museum of Natural History, Field Museum of Natural History, Peabody Museum (Harvard), Maxwell Museum of Anthropology, Museum of the American Indian,

PLATE 1. An aerial photograph of the Pueblo Bonito–Chetro Ketl area. The dots mark the position of the wall (gray-white linearity) that once extended between the two greathouses. *Photo*: University of New Mexico Southwest Cultural Resources Center.

Heye Foundation (now housed at the National Museum of the American Indian), and the library at Chaco Canyon. However, a significant number of materials are in less obvious places, though if one is familiar with the lives of Pepper, Wetherill, and other early Chacoan workers, they can be located: Pennsylvania State University, the University of Pennsylvania, the Philadelphia Museum of Art, and the Middle American Research Institute and the Latin American Library at Tulane University, among other institutions. There are also materials in private hands. It takes time, careful research, perseverance, and (relatively minimal) funding to locate these materials and to collect the data contained therein. Nevertheless, the fact that the materials are distributed among twenty-two institutions is a major reason it took so long to prepare this report.

As one example, consider the George H. Pepper papers and objects. While working at Chaco Canyon, Pepper deposited almost all the materials at the American Museum of Natural History, except objects given to the Hyde Exploring Expedition patrons B. Talbot Hyde and Frederick E. Hyde, Jr, and those relatively few objects in the hands of Richard Wetherill. In 1909, Pepper left the American Museum to become an assistant curator in the Department of American Archaeology at the University Museum at the University of Pennsylvania in Philadelphia; he was also briefly affiliated there with the Philadelphia Museum of Art. Some of his papers and objects accompanied him to Philadelphia and some remained there, including a Chacoan sandal left at the Philadelphia Museum of Art. In 1910 Pepper returned to New York City to join George G. Heye in the development of the Museum of the American Indian, Heye Foundation. He brought most of his papers and objects with him and they remained at the museum until Pepper's death on May 13, 1924, including hundreds of photographs from the Hyde Exploring Expedition work at Chaco Canyon and elsewhere.

During his career, Pepper acquired collections of mostly ethnographic objects, primarily from the Southwest but also from elsewhere in the Americas, for private individuals, e.g., Mrs. Robert (Emily J.) de Forest of New York City, one of the sponsors of the 1903 de Forest–Hyde Expedition, and also Mrs. Phoebe Apperson Hearst, mother of William Randolph Hearst and founder of the Phoebe A. Hearst Museum of Anthropology (formerly the Lowie Museum) at the University of California Berkeley (figures 3–4). Each collection contained at least five hundred to six hundred objects. The card catalogues apparently were never completed and delivered to the two women, so the exact numbers are uncertain, except for a 1903 typed and annotated inventory of the Hearst Southwestern Pottery collection that Pepper sent to cultural anthropologist A. L. Kroeber on November 15, 1905, which lists 588 objects. Furthermore, in the case of the de Forest Collection, between the time Pepper assembled it (1903) and its sale to the Pennsylvania State University (1973), it was moved at least four times between New York and Pennsylvania, during which moves some objects were lost, sold, traded, broken, or otherwise dispersed or lost.

After Pepper's premature death in 1924, his widow, Jessie Crellin Pepper, in need of money, sold the majority of his papers, Pepper's professional library, and the objects in her possession (mostly ethnographic

FIGURE 3. Phoebe Apperson Hearst, patron, philanthropist, and mother of William Randolph Hearst. Date and photographer unidentified.

FIGURE 4. (*above*) George Pepper photograph (ca. 1910) of some Santa Clara Pueblo pottery collected for Phoebe Apperson Hearst.

FIGURE 5. (*opposite above*) Richard Wetherill 1895–1896 photograph of the first Wetherill store and residence, east of Pueblo Bonito.

FIGURE 6. (*opposite below*) Richard Wetherill 1896 photograph of the second Wetherill store and permanent residence adjacent to the west side of Pueblo Bonito.

materials from the Southwest) to the newly created Middle American Research Institute at Tulane University. The Peppers had twin daughters, Gertrude and Jeanette, born in 1905. Gertrude died at age two from spinal meningitis. Jeanette Pepper later attended the University of New Mexico, where Dorothy L. Keur became her mentor in the Department of Anthropology. Keur, the author of *Big Bead Mesa* (1941), was originally an archaeologist but later became more interested in aspects of cultural anthropology. Jeanette Pepper gave Keur a small collection of her father's photographs from the work at Chaco Canyon and elsewhere in the Southwest, and Keur, in turn, deposited them with the department. (In the early 1980s, I corresponded with Keur about Jeanette Pepper and the Pepper photographs.) It was among this collection that I found the image of the *first* Wetherill store east of Pueblo Bonito (figure 5); compare this with the second Wetherill residence and trading post (figure 6) that resolved the "mystery" of the "Ohmygod site" (Reyman 1989, 45).[2] Jeanette Pepper Cameron died in 1978 at age 73.

There is more to the story of how Pepper's field records, papers, and objects became so widely dispersed, but this gives readers some basic insight into the matter. The same situation pertains to the papers of Richard Wetherill and, to a lesser extent, those of S. J. Holsinger, Edgar Lee Hewett, Warren K. Moorehead, and other late nineteenth- and early twentieth-century workers at Chaco Canyon.

QUESTIONS

The questions of population size and population density at Chaco Canyon have long been of interest to archaeologists (Reyman 1989, 49–52). Population estimates vary widely and are often based on the number of buried remains (or perceived paucity thereof) recovered from the sites and nearby areas. Bernardini (1999) and Windes (1984) are notable exceptions who rely on data from architectural features. As Akins (1986, 1–15, 151–65; 2003) indicates, the basic data for a substantial proportion of the Chacoan burials are found in archives and are unpublished. Akins's was one the most comprehensive studies and remains a valuable resource (cf., e.g., Akins 2003, Akins and Schelberg 1984, and Palkovich 1984), but

Marden's (2011) unpublished dissertation has, to some extent, superseded it. Akins (1986, 2003) and Akins and Schelberg (1984) unintentionally excluded the data for, or at least mention of, as many as several hundred additional burials excavated by Pepper and Wetherill (Pepper 1896a, 1896b, 1899a; Wetherill 1896) and perhaps also by Moorehead, none of which are published or even informally reported (Reyman 1989, 49–52).

The unpublished data regarding burials and mortuary practices discussed below have a direct bearing on these questions, as do the data regarding hearths. For example, the number of hearths at Pueblo Bonito is interpreted by some as an indicator of relatively low resident population at the site and, by extension, of low population density in the canyon (see Windes 1984). But the unpublished data indicate that a significantly greater number of hearths were found which, when combined with the unpublished mortuary data, suggests that population estimates must be revised upward.

SOME EARLY HISTORICAL BACKGROUND ON CHACOAN BURIALS

The following extended statement from Neil M. Judd (1954, 325, 340–42) provides one of the better overviews of the problem of the apparent lack of burials at Chaco Canyon, with an amusing final paragraph.

> The cemetery at Pueblo Bonito has never been found. This fact not only adds to the mystery of the ruin but limits our knowledge of its one-time occupants. With an estimated peak population of over 1,000, and with one section inhabited perhaps 250 years, Pueblo Bonito should have experienced between 4,700 and 5,400 deaths [based on Earnest Hooten's (1930, 349) estimate of an annual death rate at Pecos Pueblo of between 20 and 25 per thousand]. How the bodies were disposed of, and where, continue to be tantalizing puzzles. The only human remains thus far discovered at Pueblo Bonito had been buried within the house cluster . . . Of all the people who formerly dwelt there, young and old, we account for less than 100.

CHAPTER TWO

Where did the Bonitians bury their [estimated] 5,000 dead? The local cemetery is yet to be discovered. If our Late Bonitians adopted the burial practices of their hosts, as seems likely, the puzzle is all the greater. For, as I have explained elsewhere, the Old Bonitians were a Pueblo II people living in a Pueblo III age. One would naturally expect them to follow the recognized customs of their cultural level, including burial in trash piles near the dwellings. But they did not. Our trench through the West Court exposed a previously undisturbed portion of the old village dump. We found no burial there and none in cross sectioning the west refuse mound, composed of both Old and Late Bonitian rubbish.

Hewett (1921, p. 11)[3] supposed the area about Casa Rinconada, on the south side of the canyon, to be the common burial ground for Chettro Kettle, Pueblo Bonito, and Pueblo del Arroyo, although a quarter century earlier Pepper had ascertained that burials occurring there belonged to nearby house groups (Pepper 1920, p. 376).[4] Our own study of small-house sites throughout the Chaco district, sites varying in age from B.M. III to P. III, show [sic] that burials were frequently, but not exclusively made in the associated refuse heaps. When we come to the major villages, however, a new custom presents itself, isolation and concealment of the community burial ground.

What is true in Chaco Canyon is equally true elsewhere throughout the Anasazi area . . . no cemetery has yet been disclosed in connection with a major Pueblo III ruin.[5] A few burials, yes, but not the graveyard . . .

If failure to locate the Pueblo Bonito cemetery has bothered me more than my predecessors it is because I have probably given more thought to the matter. Pepper has searched the two associated refuse mounds; his excavations had also proved that subfloor interment was not widely practiced here. Two other possibilities remained for consideration: A burial ground somewhat removed from the village and cremation.

Mrs. John Wetherill once related to me a Kayenta Navaho explanation that accounts both for the lack of a cemetery at Pueblo Bonito and the paucity of trees on the mesas above. The Bonitians cremated their dead, said these western Navaho who had never been in Chaco Canyon, and that is why there are very few junipers and pinions [sic] remaining in the vicinity. Careful search, however, failed to disclose the burned spots and fragments of calcined bones that would lend substance to this explanation.

A negative return here reflects the findings of archaeologists, namely, that cremation was rarely, if ever, practiced by the Anasazis. The numerous cremated burials at Hawikuh are those of southern Indians who came to work for the Zuñi in pre-Spanish times (Hodge 1921).

Inasmuch as some 3 feet of sand and silt had settled over the valley floor since the abandonment of Pueblo Bonito, it seemed desirable at least to glance beneath this overburden. A half dozen test pits all proved barren. Therefore, unless we missed the cemetery completely, it lies more than a quarter mile from the ruin.[6] The greedy arroyo, whose banks we have examined after each summer rain, disclosed nothing of promise. We observed nothing to suggest the likelihood of burials in the talus at the base of the north cliff. Thus, with every reasonable possibility exhausted, we could only leave to the future the mystery of the missing cemetery.

Our Chaco Canyon visitors, however, were not so easily discouraged. My admission of defeat was to them a challenge. . . . If their proffered solutions sometimes seemed a bit ludicrous I had only to remember that my own had failed.

One theorist, for example, had the dead of Pueblo Bonito floating down the Chaco wash, one by one, on log rafts. Here again, as in the Navaho story, we have a single explanation that accounts both for our depleted forests and the absence of a communal burial graveyard. Utterly innocent of the birch-bark canoe that carried Hiawatha on his final journey, these individual rafts floated westward down the Chaco and into the San Juan; thence, into the Colorado and the Gulf of California. The alluvial fan at the mouth of the Rio Colorado is certainly one place I never thought to look for Bonitian burials.

Nevertheless, there is a curious omission in Judd's discussion: In September 1906, William Strover of the General Land Office resurveyed the central portion of Chaco Canyon from just west of Pueblo del Arroyo to just east of Chetro Ketl and across the arroyo to Casa Rinconada and the sites surrounding it. The survey was completed on September 15, 1906 and approved on November 30, 1906, and the plat map was officially filed in the US Land Office in Santa Fe on December 10, 1906. Between Pueblo Bonito and Chetro Ketl, just north of the ditch that ran on the north side of Wetherill's Reservoir, Strover marked a number of features that he labeled "Ancient Burial Mounds." Across the arroyo he drew a large circular structure labeled "Ancient Estufa" with "burial mounds" on the east, south, and west sides.

This "large circular structure" is Casa Rinconada, and at least some of the burial mounds are the Bc or Hosta Butte Phase sites (although as will be shown later, there were also burial mounds there). But what about those features—"ancient burial mounds"—on the north side of the canyon? They are located, at least in part, in the area of the Hillside Ruin that Judd partially excavated (Judd 1964, 146–53). Did Strover mistake the debris covering the Hillside Ruin for burial mounds? What also makes this matter curious is that a copy of this map is among Judd's papers at the National Anthropological Archives (one of the few but important unpublished records of his that I found). Judd knew of Strover's assertions, yet he never mentioned the map even in passing in any of his published writings. Nor did Pepper, who must certainly have known of its existence; it was a follow-up to S. J. Holsinger's 1901 survey, and Pepper knew about Holsinger's report because it effectively ended the Hyde Exploring Expedition work in Chaco. Other fieldworkers concerned with the problem of Chaco burials—Hewett and Senter and, more recently, Hayes, Akins, and Windes—do not mention Strover's map, even to dismiss its identification as an early example of misidentifying small house mounds for burial mounds (e.g., Akins 1986, 15).

To return to the question of the location of expected Chacoan burials, if Judd was puzzled, even mystified, by what was to him a paucity of burials, others before and after were no less baffled. As Hewett (1936b, 115, 118) wrote fifteen years after the 1921 comment cited above by Judd:

The mortuary practice of the Chaqueños is a profound mystery. In all the excavating that has been done, and in the diligent prospecting carried on for fifteen years, no general cemetery has been found. Two or three burials in a place, such as the large refuse heap of Chetro Ketl; the talus slope behind the pueblo; the débris around Casa Rinconada and in the small house sites nearby; in small house mounds in the "Gap" through which the canyon is entered [more about these particular mounds later]; in the talus near Hungo Pavi—these constitute our finds in skeletal remains[.] Pepper's field notes, the Hyde Expedition, describe thirty burials from Pueblo Bonito and small sites excavated.[7] No convincing evidence of cremation has been found. Yet, Chaco Canyon supported thousands of people for three or four centuries at least. We don't give it up, but we are thoroughly mystified. All that can be said at present is that the dead were buried in very casual and miscellaneous ways, as, in refuse heaps, under rock débris, occasionally in house rooms, a few in small burial mounds; usually quite near the surface, in flexed position, without regular orientation.

From this and other statements, Akins (1986, 13) suggests, "Hewett appears to have been the first to ask why there were so few Chaco burials instead of asking, with his predecessors, where the burials were." I am not convinced that Akins is correct in her assessment of Hewett because Hewett notes in the same volume (1936, 51–52):

> Along the important ten miles of the Chaco Canyon with its great central group and a large community house on each mile of the north side of the valley, not a refuse heap is to be seen that has not been dug over, and across the valley to the south where the dead from the great communities were once supposed to have been buried, not a mound can be found that has not been pitted over and over in search of pottery. The principal museum collections in America have been secured by purchase from unscientific collectors working in this way.

Although Hewett implies here that the south side of the canyon is not, in fact, the locus of the cemeteries for "the great communities," his statement does not seem to be that of one who questions why there were so few burials but rather an explanation for the then-current paucity of them. Reading the same material, Akins and I interpret Hewett's statements quite differently, a point to which I return later.

Akins (1986, 13) further notes, "This theme was carried on by Donovan Senter," who wrote:

> Ever since the first excavations were begun in Chaco ruins, archaeologists have wondered at the amazing dearth of burials there. The canyon was the home of thousands of people at one time, as is proved by the number of rooms of the same building date in the large pueblos, and an archaeologist acquainted with the burial customs of the northern prehistoric Southwestern Pueblo people would expect to find thousands of graves. Instead, entire seasons have passed without the uncovering of a single skeleton, and the locations of sixteen at Tseh So in 1936, fragmentary as they were, was reason for rejoicing (Senter 1937a, 141).

While Senter does question why there were so few burials, it is implicit in his account that one would expect to find a large number of burials and, therefore, to wonder where they are. There is no rejection of the idea that they must be somewhere within the canyon or its immediate environs. Senter believed that one or more cemeteries lay deeply buried beneath alluvial fill, and trenches were cut to expose these. The search was unsuccessful, but Senter remained optimistic: "Whatever burials may have been made in the canyon floor must await uncovering by teams and scrapers or by another period of erosion." He further notes on the same page (1937a, 142):

> To the southwest of Chaco Canyon but in the Chaco culture district, a cemetery was pilfered a few years ago by the Navajos and the vessels sold to a trader. The pottery indicated its period as

Pueblo III and possibly Pueblo II as well. No large ruin was near, but potsherd areas were found on the surfaces of low mounds near the burials. The principal reason for supposing that the ancient people of the Chaco buried their dead in cemeteries on the canyon floor is that this was the general custom for the majority of people in the northern part of the Pueblo area.

Presumably, the canyon floor would have included low mounds as cemeteries. Senter was a strong advocate of trenching the canyon to determine the depth and extent of alluvial deposition, the rate of deposition, and erosion sequences, and to locate burial grounds and other cultural features:

> Linked with the problem of old land surfaces was that of burials, which have been notable for their scarcity in this canyon, and it seemed that an investigation of these old surfaces might yield some information on the possibility of burial grounds deep below the present surface. To this end, the 1936 University of New Mexico field school implemented a project to allow cutting of one unit of a trench that will eventually cross-section the canyon. This section of the canyon is to be extended, eventually, from cliff wall to cliff wall along the line of projected stations.
>
> Station 1 was set up four feet from the south wall enclosing the great sanctuary of Chetro Ketl.[8] From this point a line was run thirty degrees east of south to the edge of the arroyo, 1164 feet distant. Cut 1 was begun between points 250 and 300 feet south of Station 1. This cut, fifty feet long and twelve feet wide, was carried down six feet through the surface sand. At this depth the excavation was narrowed down to a width of six feet, and the length was shortened to twenty-five feet, between points 250 and 275 feet from Station 1. The trench was carried down another six feet. The excavation was then narrowed to three feet wide and carried down six feet, giving a vertical face eighteen feet below the surface and twenty-five feet long.[9] At the bottom was sand showing no trace of cultural material (Senter 1937b, 68–69).

The work stopped at this point. Senter's figure 9 (1937b, 70) shows the location of Cut 1, and figure 10 (73) shows the cut in cross-section and the stratigraphy in it. No burial ground was encountered, or even individual burials, but Senter did not expect such on the north side of the arroyo; rather, they presumably were deeply buried across the arroyo on the south side of the canyon.

Trenching the canyon was an interesting idea, though impractical using hand labor. Cut 1 was not expanded in later field schools, and other cuts along the line of projected stations were apparently never attempted. With modern excavation equipment, the project is technically feasible but at a prohibitive cost and with substantial damage to the land. Ground-penetrating radar offers the possibility of finding large burial areas several meters deep, if such exist, but to the best of my knowledge a project with this aim has not been attempted at Chaco.

Later workers have continued to focus on the problem of Chacoan burials, or lack thereof. Alden Hayes et al. write (1981, 61):

> One of the more intriguing mysteries of Chaco Canyon is the relative absence of burials associated with Bonito Phase houses. Burial customs in the Hosta Butte Phase were unchanged from earlier times in the Chaco and following the general Anasazi pattern of burying flexed bodies in the refuse, under the floors of rooms, or, less frequently, on the floors of abandoned rooms. To date, about 325 burials have been excavated in the canyon—only about one-third of them from the great houses, even though much more fill has been removed from those sites, and not all these pertained to the Bonito phase.

Hayes et al. (1981, 62) cite Judd's previously mentioned estimate that Pueblo Bonito should have experienced between 4,700 and 5,400 deaths in an assumed 250-year occupation of the pueblo. The 1981 study does not give an estimated number of deaths but provides population estimates of 2,889 people during the Hosta Butte Phase and 2,763 during the Bonito Phase, for a total of 5,652 people (Hayes et al. 1981, 51). Several years later, Tom Windes (1984, 83–84) estimated the maximum population of Pueblo Bonito at one hundred and that for the entire canyon at perhaps two thousand; Stephen Lekson (1984b, 272) puts the total population at 2,100–2,700. Perhaps the latest and lowest estimate for Pueblo Bonito is Wesley Bernardini's (1999). Based on what he calls "residential suites" or "households," Bernardini states that no more than twelve such units housing about seventy people were occupied simultaneously. Presumably, he would also lower the population estimates for Chetro Ketl, Pueblo del Arroyo, Hungo Pavi, and the other great houses.

Regardless of which of these, if any, is ultimately correct, even the lowest population estimate during the time Chaco Canyon was occupied should have produced far more than the 325 burials noted by Hayes or the approximately seven hundred individuals listed by Akins (1986, 9, 153–65). Akins (1986, 15), however, makes two points: first,

> While most larger sites in the Southwest are just that, large sites with many occupants, the great houses in Chaco appear to have housed relatively few persons, possibly elites [cf. Akins and Schelberg 1984; Plog and Heitman 2010; Windes 1984, 84]. Certainly, a maximum population of 100 at Pueblo Bonito would leave fewer burials than would the 1,100 population suggested by Judd.

And second,

> There is excavation bias. Excavation at the small sites has usually concentrated on architectural features and consequently has missed all or most of the midden internments. The burial mounds referred to by early explorers were the trash middens associated with the small sites.

Akins restates and expands upon this in a later paper (2003, 100):

> My previous research on Pueblo Bonito has been in the context of burials excavated from Chaco Canyon (Akins 1986). I have

compared great houses and small site burials in order to draw conclusions about how Chacoan society was organized. Much of the burial information for small sites is incomplete, and it has a significant bias toward room excavations. Midden burials are commonly disturbed or lack information on associated ceramics, making them difficult to place chronologically. As a result, our current knowledge of Chacoan burial practices may not represent the entire range.

I agree with Akins that excavations at the small sites focused on architecture. This is a practice seen not only at Chaco but elsewhere in the Southwest in the first half of the twentieth century. However, it is important to note that the trash middens at both Bc-50 and Bc-51 were excavated and reported on (Brand et al. 1937; Kluckhohn and Reiter 1939). Moreover, as discussed below and illustrated with photographs, although some so-called burial mounds were indeed trash middens associated with small sites, the unpublished records make it clear that other mounds were, in fact, burial mounds and not trash middens. It is similarly clear from these records that Pepper and Wetherill excavated burial mounds or cemeteries, per se.

Finally, one might argue that Pepper, Hewett, Judd, and others, working from the assumption of a large Chacoan population, expected to find large numbers of burials. That they did not was explained, in some cases, by their simply not looking in the right places, or not digging deep enough or widely enough. This certainly seems true in the case of Donovan Senter. Furthermore, when they did not find anything approaching the expected burials, they did not change their basic assumption but resolved to look elsewhere.

This makes sense except for one fact: as discussed below and demonstrated in their notes and photographs, Pepper and Wetherill did find large numbers of burials. But they did not publish their findings because, at least in the case of one large burial mound just to the west-southwest of Pueblo del Arroyo (Mound 5), the grave goods were few and of little of interest to them. What became of these skeletal remains and the accompanying artifacts is a question that is considered later in this volume.

THE CASE FOR THE UNPUBLISHED RECORD

It is almost axiomatic that archaeologists never publish all the data from their fieldwork. There are numerous reasons for this: e.g., the data analyses and write-up lag far behind the excavation, archaeologists take on new projects before completion of the old ones, and publishers often limit the length of books and articles (Reyman 1971, passim; Reyman 1989, 41–45). It is also probably true that the larger the project, the more likely some or even a sizable portion of the data produced never find their way into print. The Teotihuacán Mapping Project dealing with the Central Valley of Mexico is a case in point: its important findings remain unpublished in full. This is one reason the efforts of Frances Joan Mathien and her colleagues to publish the results of the work of the Chaco Center are so important and appreciated (Akins 1986; Cully 1985; Mathies and Winden 1987; McKenna and Truell 1986; Toll and McKenna 1997).

The Chaco Digital Initiative (CDI) housed at the University of Virginia is making much of the unpublished record for Chaco available, both texts and notably its photographic archive, as well as compiling an archive of published materials.[10] It is a work in progress and a valuable contribution to Chacoan archaeology. It originally had a scheduled completion date of late 2009, but clearly it is larger than initially contemplated because as of this writing (2024), there is still work to be done: the CDI is an ongoing project. The CDI also contains records for related sites such as Aztec Ruin. Curiously, although CDI researchers visited many of the same institutions that Martin Nickels and I did, such as the American Museum of Natural History and the Middle American Research Institute, they either overlooked some of the unpublished records (e.g., Pepper's 1896–1899 field notes, Pepper's 1899 lecture, and Wetherill's 1896 field notes and 1904–1905 letters) and photographs (the latter include some Pepper–Wetherill shots of burial mounds and burial images discussed in this book, as well as the rest of the Pepper–Wetherill images from Chaco Canyon that are at the MARI at Tulane), or perhaps these have not yet been posted in the bibliography and gallery on the CDI website.

The problem of unpublished data is not, of course, limited to archaeology. Unpublished data exist for all the subdisciplines of anthropology. One example in linguistics is some six hundred boxes of John P. Harrington's notes on the native languages of California that apparently remain unedited and unpublished (Starn 2004, 137). Most large and medium-sized museums, research institutions, libraries, and archives similarly contain substantial and significant amounts of unpublished field notes, photographs, maps, sketches, audio-visual records, and more. In addition to archaeological materials, my research on Chaco Canyon has turned up substantial and important unpublished data on human skeletal remains, faunal and floral data, Pueblo and Navajo ethnography (including word lists and other linguistic information), the history of ethnography and archaeology in the Southwest, local history, and early efforts at applied anthropology. An untold wealth of information is awaiting interested scholars, and at a time when fieldwork is increasingly expensive and sometimes difficult to undertake, especially in archaeology, these materials represent major untapped or underutilized sources of primary data.

The unpublished Chaco Canyon data are important because they make us rethink a series of issues: the history of ancient Chaco and the history of Chacoan archaeology; the estimates of population and population density that have changed greatly over time, and have trended sharply downward in recent decades from thousands of ancient Chacoans to a few hundred, or even lower (the deserted ceremonial center hypothesis); a reevaluation of the excavation techniques used by Pepper, Wetherill, and others during the Hyde Exploring Expedition's 1896–1901 tenure at Chaco; and the ethics, morality, and practices of the HEE and some later archaeologists with regard to the handling and preservation of skeletal remains.

Some of the unpublished data from Pueblo Bonito are discussed below. Most are from George H. Pepper and Richard A. Wetherill's field notes from the Hyde Exploring Expedition, and some were discussed earlier in Reyman 1989 and other published papers. They receive fuller attention here, particularly the field records and photographs from Rooms 32 and 33 at Pueblo Bonito and Chaco mounds and burials. Additional attention is paid to the work of Neil M. Judd and Frank H. H. Roberts, Jr., both published and unpublished. These records cover a variety of subjects—architectural features such as hearths and room construction, burial mounds and excavated burials, grave goods, various artifacts, plant materials—which, in turn, affect our understanding of the archaeological history of Chaco Canyon, provide new and added information on mortuary practices, and suggest that recent estimates of ancient Chacoan populations are too low.

PEPPER, WETHERILL, AND MOOREHEAD: ETHICS, MORALITY, AND PRACTICES

This is an appropriate place to discuss one of the important issues mentioned immediately above—the ethics, morality, and practices of Pepper, Wetherill, and Moorehead with regard to the handling and preservation of skeletal remains. While we don't know precisely what these three men thought about skeletal remains—none of them specifically addresses them as former humans except for a joking reference by Pepper to a skull he encountered as "poor Yoric[k]" while working in Rooms 32–33—it's fair to say that, unlike many modern-day Native Americans and others, they did not consider the remains sacred nor treat them as such. When I was a curator at the Illinois State Museum, we repatriated some of the affiliated remains we held—"some" because for various reasons not all native people wanted them back—by placing them in cedar boxes, at the tribes' request, and giving them to the Peoria and other tribes for reburial on their lands. I believe such an idea would have been unthinkable to Pepper, Wetherill, and Moorehead.

As discussed below, Pepper was several decades in the forefront of using stratigraphy in his Pueblo Bonito excavations (figure 8, below), a technique usually credited to Nels Nelson (1914, 1916) at Galisteo Basin sites. Pepper also kept voluminous field notes in his diaries. (Wetherill's field notes are much briefer.) Both Pepper and Wetherill took hundreds, perhaps more than a thousand photographs, a significant expense that the Hyde brothers paid. Moorehead (1907), in his 1896 "hit-and-run" session at Chaco, apparently took few if any notes and few photographs and collected three (?) skulls from burials, some pottery, and other artifacts. His "fieldwork" was little more than vandalism.

As for ethics and morality, Wetherill and Moorehead sold objects they excavated and otherwise collected; Pepper, by contrast, seems to have sold *only* ethnographic objects such as Santa Clara pottery, Navajo blankets and weaving tools, and copper jewelry. However, all three men apparently had no compunction or even the slightest remorse about discarding human skeletal remains, as Pepper and Wetherill did at Chaco by throwing them into the Chaco Arroyo behind Mound 5. Moorehead collected three ancient Chacoan crania (57024A, 57033A, 57049A) with violent perimortem trauma (large puncture wounds), but he did not bother with or discarded the postcranial remains. (One would like to know what their Navajo fieldworkers thought of this practice.) It's worth noting that Professor Frederick Ward Putnam, the official director of the Hyde Exploring Expedition, does not seem to have raised an objection to Pepper and Wetherill's disposal of skeletal remains or to Moorehead's brief work at Chaco Canyon; at least no extant letter or report states that he did. Theirs was a "typical practice and attitude" of the late nineteenth to early twentieth centuries. By comparison, late eighteenth to early nineteenth-century "archaeologists"/vandals such as Giovanni Belzoni (1778–1823) thought nothing of tearing away Egyptian mummy wrappings to find offerings secreted within them, both small preciosities and papyrus scrolls.

Most archaeologists today are appalled by such behavior—the lack of both professional ethics and morality—and rightly so; I am, but this seems to have been the norm for the time and not restricted to Pepper, Wetherill, and Moorehead. Today such behavior would be neither tolerated nor accepted, and recent experience indicates that sanctions fall on those who engage in it. It's actions such as these and the absence of underlying ethics and morality that underpin much of Native American opposition to archaeology—which the tribes often see as little more than illegal and disrespectful "grave-digging"—and that led, in part, to the Native American Graves Protection and Repatriation Act in which I participated as a Curator of Anthropology at the Illinois State Museum.[11]

Though it was not S. J. Holsinger's *stated* intent as a special agent for Congress, one major effect of his 1901 report was to end the Hyde Exploring Expedition's work at Chaco Canyon, which was planned to last at least a couple of years longer. His report also eventually led directly to the establishment of Chaco Canyon as a national monument.

CHAPTER THREE

Pueblo Bonito and Chaco Canyon

The Unpublished Record

THE UNPUBLISHED RECORD FOR Pueblo Bonito differs in magnitude from that for Chaco Canyon in general: as far as I know, there is more unpublished material for Pueblo Bonito than for any other Chacoan site, and the significance of the unpublished material in terms of our understanding of Pueblo Bonito is correspondingly greater than is the case for any other site there.

There are good reasons for this: Pueblo Bonito is the largest site in Chaco Canyon in terms of the number of rooms and is the most thoroughly excavated (although I've argued since 1971 [Reyman 1971] that there are substantial undisturbed subterranean deposits). The artifact assemblage is much richer than those from the other major excavated sites such as Chetro Ketl (although Chetro Ketl has some spectacular materials, e.g., the wooden ritual objects as reported by Vivian et al. 1978 and the shell, turquoise, and jet necklaces from the sealed Great Sanctuary wall niches (Vivian and Reiter 1960). Together with Pueblo Alto, Pueblo del Arroyo, and Chetro Ketl, Pueblo Bonito is considered by some archaeologists to be the center of the Chacoan "system"—the Chacoan world.

Neil Judd, the field director for the 1921–1927 archaeological fieldwork sponsored by the National Geographic Society, published two large volumes on Pueblo Bonito, the first on "material culture" (Judd 1954) and the second on architecture (Judd 1964). A third volume was planned on the pottery of Pueblo Bonito, to be written by Frank H. H. Roberts, Jr. (Judd 1954, 184). Roberts did the basic ceramic study as his PhD dissertation (Roberts 1927), and although this was eventually published posthumously (Roberts 1991), the major volume on Chaco ceramics, as envisioned by Roberts and Judd, was never published as such. Thus, despite all the work done and published on Pueblo Bonito, we do not have a definitive major study of the ceramics from the site, though some of Roberts's data are apparently included in Toll and McKenna (1997). Similarly, although we have excellent photographs and drawings of some of the ceramics excavated earlier by Pepper and Wetherill for the Hyde Exploring Expedition (Pepper 1920), there is no real ceramic analysis in Pepper's site report. His discussion of pottery types, per se, is limited to one page (164) and two figures (69 and 70).[1]

Roberts (1927, 40–41) also notes the former existence of a third Great Sanctuary in the west plaza of Pueblo Bonito. Judd (1954, 176–77; 1964, passim) refers to it but provides relatively few details. "It does not appear on any published ground plans," wrote Gordon Vivian and Paul Reiter (1960, 71), and these two authors add little information regarding it, although they note it could have been used contemporaneously with the other two Great Sanctuaries (Great Kiva A and Great Kiva Q).

One additional factor must be mentioned: the general tendency of scholars to accept what they read as true, particularly statements of methodology, technique, and procedure. It is sometimes the case, however, that the published record is not true or that, at best, it is incomplete. This is demonstrated in the following statement by Clark Wissler in his Foreword to Pepper's *Pueblo Bonito*:

> The author [Pepper] long delayed the preparation of this report in the hopes that further work could be taken up at the ruin and that a more exhaustive study . . . could be prosecuted; but as neither of these desirable extensions of the work now seems possible, he has decided to issue his notes in their present form as a record of what he has done . . . Finally, . . . what is published here are his field notes supplemented by descriptive data for the most important specimens. The author is to be commended for . . . placing before us *his field record in full* (In Pepper 1920, 2; emphasis added).

As noted previously (Reyman 1989, 44), many archaeologists accepted Wissler's statement as true; I did not for several reasons, not the least of which are limits imposed by publishers, which mean that archaeologists usually do not publish all of their data. This is confirmed by, for example, a comparison of Pepper's published and unpublished descriptions of the architecture of Room 75 at Pueblo Bonito. The first of these (Pepper 1920, 262) is as follows: "Room 75 is of circular form and lies between Rooms 68 and 72. Owing to the fact that this room was a typical estufa [kiva], no description of it will be given (Figure 106)."

Pepper's (1896b) unpublished field notes (the pages are usually unnumbered) provide the following additional architectural details that add considerably to the description and to the complexity of the architecture and its context. I have provided some punctuation and capitalization for clarity. Pepper often omitted periods at the ends of sentences and did not always begin new sentences with capitals, but no words have been changed or omitted, and I have not corrected grammatical and other errors but have changed spelling in accordance with modern usage, e.g., fireplace for Pepper's fire place. Here, then, is his account of Room 75 from his 1896 field notes:

> Small estufa has eight supports—on bench—wall composed of small thick slabs well laid has been well plastered some of which still remains on N.E. part—Eastern part of bench still retains its plaster—at the Eastern side the plaster has been removed or had fallen, and a thin coat had been applied to the space between the thick plaster. The beams in the support were about a foot in diameter. There was an angular jog in the South side but none in the North. There was a fireplace in the centre of the estufa or rather S. of its centre. It was built of stones and was plastered, and the interior was red, probably from paint. Running S.W. from the fireplace was an airshaft built of stones. Under the floor was a series of angular rooms, a large one at the N.E. side, which was quite deep—a shallow one at the Western side, which was only a foot deep but had a deeper place at the N. & S. ends. There was another at the SE side which was also deep—the intervening space was solid masonry as near as could be ascertained without tearing it down.

The accompanying photograph in *Pueblo Bonito*, labeled Figure 106 (Pepper 1920, 259), shows the fireplace but none of the subfloor rooms. The roof supports are not all visible, and despite Pepper's statement that this was a "typical estufa," the fact is that the number of roof supports (usually four to six) varies from one kiva to another: there were eight in this presumed kiva. The fireplace is not mentioned in the published description, nor is it referenced in the Index, either by architectural feature or page number. Therefore, a count made of the number of fireplaces (hearths) using *only* the Index or published room descriptions excludes the fireplace in Room 75. The same problem exists for fireplaces and other architectural features for numerous other rooms at Pueblo Bonito. The unpublished field notes and other documents contain significantly more primary data than are found in the published record, notably in the number of hearths. This is important because some archaeologists (e.g., Windes 1984) base their population estimates for Pueblo Bonito on the number of hearths found at the site.

Wissler, in fact, knew that Pepper had not written up all his data. In a letter to Pepper dated December 18, 1918 (on file at the American Museum of Natural History), Wissler acknowledges that the manuscript is *only part of the total record of Pueblo Bonito*. Yet in his Foreword published in 1920, Wissler makes no mention that some of the record is omitted. Instead, as cited above, he states that the published report is the "record in full" of Pepper's work at Pueblo Bonito.

Why the apparent contradiction? It is an interesting but ultimately unanswerable question, though two possible answers come to mind. First, Wissler knew that others such as Warren K. Moorehead and Richard Wetherill had worked at the site, and he may have known (or assumed) that there were still unpublished materials from *their* work but not from Pepper himself. Moorehead does not seem to have had many more, if any, Pueblo Bonito materials and did not publish anything more on the site or on Chaco Canyon before his death in 1939. Indeed, about one-third of his 1906 publication on Pueblo Bonito is material taken directly from Pepper (1905). Other portions are taken from his own letters and previously published papers by others, all of which suggests that Moorehead had relatively few notes and photographs from his brief April 1897 fieldwork at Chaco Canyon. But if Wissler assumed there were unpublished materials aside from Pepper's, he was correct. Wetherill never had the chance to publish his Chaco Canyon field records. In 1910 he was apparently murdered from ambush by a Navajo man, Chis-chillin-Begay, in what is said to have been a dispute over horses or cattle. The matter has never been satisfactorily resolved. Wetherill's field records contain significant data on sites, burials, and other excavated materials (Reyman 1989, 50–51).

Another possibility is that Wissler thought Pepper had indeed included all his material in the final draft of the Pueblo Bonito manuscript, as he indicates in his Foreword. (He could have checked this by comparing the two manuscripts, of course, but apparently did not.) If this was the case, then he was incorrect, as the following section further demonstrates.

SOME KEY OMISSIONS FROM PEPPER'S PUBLICATIONS

There is much that Pepper omitted from *Pueblo Bonito* and from his earlier reports such as Pepper 1905 and his report on Rooms 32–33 (Pepper 1909). The following are several examples that directly affect current interpretations about the site and provide an indication of the variety of unpublished materials. These include the number of hearths, the number of burials, and the contents and context of Rooms 32 and 33.

Pueblo Bonito Hearths

During the past thirty to forty years, there have been a number of reevaluations of Chacoan population size (e.g., Akins 1986; Bernardini 1999; Durand 2003; Lekson 1984b; Vivian 1990; Windes 1984, 1987, 1993). Most of these studies suggest that the ancient population was much smaller than previously estimated: Windes (1984), for example, suggests a *maximum* population of two thousand for Chaco Canyon at the height of the occupation (the late AD 1000s) and further suggests that the occupation "was, perhaps, at times intermittent or seasonal" (84).

This argument, when combined with the suggestion that the towns or great houses were occupied by elites (Akins and Schelberg 1984;

Windes 1984, 84; Plog and Heitman 2010; Gruner 2017), suggests a scenario resembling the "deserted ceremonial center" hypothesis once favored for the Maya, which has since been rejected. I argued previously (Reyman 1987, 150) that this concept was never valid for the Maya. (It is no longer accepted by most Mayanists.) Nor is it valid for Chaco, in large part because of the *unpublished* data.

These reevaluations of the Chacoan population size are based on various data, e.g., room size and usage, estimates of labor needed to construct sites, loci of pottery production, the *apparent* shortage of hearths in rooms, and the *apparent* paucity of burials within the canyon and its immediate environs. In the cases of the hearths and burials, the arguments are based largely on *negative* data and are affected significantly by the unpublished record in that the shortage of hearths and paucity of burials are more apparent than real (Reyman 1987, 1989). It is because the later studies base their population estimates, in part, on the number of hearths at Pueblo Bonito that Pepper's lack of publication about *all* the hearths excavated at the site by the Hyde Exploring Expedition is, in retrospect, a key omission.

Room size and usage are also dependent largely on the published record. As shown above, this record is also often incomplete and, therefore, is also often misleading. Perhaps ironically, Windes (1984, 77) explicitly recognizes there are problems in the published record: "Those [heating pits] at . . . Pueblo Bonito are often difficult to discern based on the available data, and I suspect that most went unrecorded." One factor Windes uses to calculate his revised population estimate is the type of hearth he classifies as a "firepit," for which his sample size at Pueblo Bonito is forty-three (Windes 1984, 77). Judd, (1954, 45), however, states that there were fifty-nine hearths in forty-eight ground-floor rooms, and Judd's figure does not include those rooms with hearths excavated by Pepper. A careful reading of Pepper (1920) indicates that there were another thirty-two hearths (using Windes' [1984, 76–77] definition) in the rooms excavated by the Hyde Exploring Expedition, and the unpublished data from Pepper's 1896 work increases this number to at least forty. Furthermore, the Hyde Exploring Expedition work continued on Pueblo Bonito for three more years, though not on the same scale as in 1896, and there are additional firepits in the unpublished field notes from this later work.

Windes himself (1997, 88) notes, "Recorded feature information is a large missing component of the early work, but no more so than for the excavations that followed for the next 60 years." Yet he does not seem to compensate for this—take it into account—in his population estimates. Thus, it was unclear to me why Windes limited his sample to forty-three; my thought was that perhaps the data required for his analysis (Windes 1984, 77) were available for only forty-three of the ninety-one firepits reported in the published literature.

I sent an email to Windes asking about this disparity, especially between the forty-three hearths that he used and the fifty-nine in Judd's published report. Windes replied via email (March 15, 2010):

> Hmmm, now that was a while ago. I believe I went to Judd's book and scanned it for mention of FPs, like those under the room notes. He may have said one thing in the text and another in the room notes in the back of the architecture volume [Judd 1964]. I may have discarded those FP's in rooms that were not really rooms (like odd triangle corners or such that got "room" designations but were not truly rooms). The archives at the Chaco Archives may have my notes from that work but I'll bet it would be hard to find. I may also (probably) [have] dumped the kiva firepits out of the totals (again, these are not rooms despite what Lekson says).

Three comments on Windes's response come to mind. First, the firepits in the "odd triangle corners or such" may have been in lower-level rooms that were built over during remodeling of a portion of the site. Or if the vertical distance between the two was sufficient, they might have been used simultaneously. Second, it is widely reported and clear in the ethnographic literature that among the Hopi, Zuni, and other Pueblos, kivas frequently serve as living quarters for men during ceremonial periods and for young, unmarried men and boys at other times. Of course, those living in kivas some of the time do not increase village population, but the fact that they live in kivas, even on a short-term basis, indicates that kivas are rooms, though not exclusively or even primarily habitation rooms. However, this probably explains how Windes arrived at the number of firepits in his study. Third, and most important, Windes's use of forty-three firepits excludes those excavated and reported by Pepper (1920) and those in his unpublished field notes.

Therefore, when one considers both the published and unpublished reports, there were more than one hundred firepits present at Pueblo Bonito (though not necessarily all used contemporaneously), or about one for every three to four ground-floor rooms. Furthermore, there were also firepits in upper-story rooms—e.g., Room 92 (Pepper 1920, 298–99)—though the total number of these is unclear from the records. Mindeleff (1891, 104) recorded the presence of fireplaces inside upper-story rooms at Hopi, although he notes that most cooking was done on the terraces. The use of upper-floor firepits is an old architectural feature that must be a factor in population estimates; using only ground-floor firepits is not sufficient. In summary, the apparent shortage of firepits is just that—*apparent* and not real (Reyman 1989, 51)—and, to the extent that this affects Windes's or other population estimates, it would seem that those estimates must be revised upward accordingly (cf. Windes 1987, 383–406).

Pueblo Bonito Kivas

This is a convenient place for a discussion of kivas or, perhaps more properly, the concept of kivas, which has long bedeviled archaeologists in the Southwest. This discussion is necessary because presumed kivas are a factor in the size of habitation units and thus some population estimates (e.g., Bernardini 1999). As noted above, Windes (2010) disagreed, and presumably still disagrees with Lekson on this subject: "I may also (probably) [have] dumped the kiva firepits out of the totals (again, these are not rooms despite what Lekson says)."

Even the basic terminology has changed. Pepper and other early workers initially used *estufa* (a Spanish word that means something akin to oven because in Spain it was a heated room in which wine was stored), though not exclusively. Pepper used "estufa" and "kiva" more or less interchangeably. Today, I know of no scholar who uses "estufa" except in a past historical reference.

Nevertheless, for more than one hundred years the term "kiva" has been problematical, not as a word, per se, but in terms of its referent: *what exactly is a kiva?* One focus topic of the 1927 Pecos Conference was how to define it. After two days of discussion, these noted scholars could not agree. As Anne Axtell Morris (1934, 38–39) wrote:

> I remember an occasion when the cream of Southwestern practicing archaeologists were gathered in one spot at a given time and spent two priceless days of their conjunction arguing on "When is a kiva not a kiva?" They not only failed to agree on that negative definition but, what was an infinitely greater loss, they never decided positively what a kiva is. And this, be it to their shame and discomfiture, when every man, woman, and child of them instantly recognize a kiva as far away as it can be seen.

As much as I admire Morris's work, her conclusion just isn't accurate, though it does bring to mind the late Supreme Court Associate Justice Potter Stewart's comment: "I could never succeed in intelligibly [defining pornography], but I know it when I see it."

One of the earliest definitions of a kiva comes from Mindeleff (1891, 111), building on what he saw as a continuum from the ancient to the ethnographic: "The chambers are distinguished from typical dwelling rooms by their size and position, and, generally in ancient examples, by their circular form."

This is also incorrect. First, pre-contact so-called kivas are round, square, rectangular, D-shaped, and sometimes eccentric in shape when they were built in the confines of a rock shelter or other location that placed physical restrictions on their construction. The Mesa Verde–style keyhole-shaped kiva has never really seemed round to me in the same way that Chacoan kivas are. And what do we make of "tower kivas" such as the "G-kivas" of Chetro Ketl (Miller 1937)? My research among the Pueblos indicates that post-contact or ethnographic kivas also come in a variety of shapes, mostly round in the Rio Grande area but square and rectangular as one transitions to the western Pueblos. Furthermore, in both areas, kivas can be above ground, as in the Eastern Pueblos and at Hotevilla and some other Hopi villages, and in a few cases subterranean and semisubterranean, as at Walpi. At Acoma there is a rectangular, above-ground kiva, but the structure, part of a room block, is built atop a round kiva, the upper wall of which is visible within the kiva. This was presumably done to hide it from the Spanish, and it may be but one example of several the Acoma camouflaged in this way, as well as at other Pueblos who were under threat from Spanish missionaries with military support.

Of course, there is one way to get a post-contact or ethnographic definition of a kiva: ask the Pueblos and then look at the features, as Frank Hamilton Cushing, J. Walter Fewkes, Alexander Stephen, and Matilda Coxe Stevenson, among others, did during their years at various Pueblos. In many cases, these early investigators provided drawings of the interiors and their contents, though often not with the consent of the people themselves.

Watson Smith tried hard to define kivas; indeed, he spent a significant portion of his research working on the problem through excavation and subsequent analyses (Smith 1952a, 1952b). In "When is a Kiva?" his seminal chapter in his Big Hawk Valley report (1952a, 154), he began by noting, "There are many pitfalls for the unwary Southwesternist, but perhaps the easiest to fall into and the most difficult to climb out of is that of the kiva." He then added a detailed trait list taken from Judd (1930), comparing kivas, dwelling rooms, and unidentified rooms for Betatakin at the Navajo National Monument in Arizona. From this, Smith made several observations:

> First, there were no circular rooms at Betatakin, so if there were kivas at all they must have been rectangular. Secondly, the five alleged kivas have only one characteristic in common to all of them, namely plastered walls. Four of them also possessed firepits, deflectors, and a ventilator hole in the wall, and it is very likely (but not stated) that the fifth, Room 55, also had those features since Judd thought it was "obviously a ceremonial chamber. Like other Betatakin kivas, its special function is evidenced by certain furnishings never present in secular structures." Moreover, its walls were smoked (Judd 1930, 35–36).

Interestingly, none of the Betatakin kivas had a *sipapu*, though one of the "unidentified rooms" did (Smith 1952a, figure 3.1 from Judd 1930, 35–36).

A sipapu is often considered an essential feature of a kiva (see, e.g., Lekson 1988, 224). In fact, in some individual Pueblo structures, kivas have *two* sipapus. Some forty years ago, a Pueblo friend and colleague explained to me that the first sipapu is the opening in the kiva floor which is connected to the Underworld and through which the spirits of the Underworld enter the kiva. He then went on to say that when they exit the kiva, via a ladder, for example, the kiva itself serves as a second sipapu. Like most things ceremonial, in my experience, sipapus are not simple features but complex ones with layers of meaning.

Smith, however, further noted: "But when we investigate the fifteen alleged 'dwelling rooms' we will see that a good many of them possess one or several or, in some cases, all of those same characteristics." He concluded, "I am convinced that no workable definition or trait list can be compiled on the basis of present knowledge whereby a kiva can certainly be recognized in the western San Juan area, at least during Pueblo II and early Pueblo III" (Lekson 1988, 224). And, at the end of "When is a Kiva?" Smith reiterated his earlier point:

> In recapitulation, then, it seems to me that the certain determination of any given structure as a kiva during Pueblo II and early Pueblo III in the San Francisco Mountain area [and presumably elsewhere?] is a well-nigh impossible task, but reasonable hypothetical identifications can be made by a broad consideration of the morphological features of the room in connection with its positional relationships (74).

I would note, "Yes, but not always, or, as Shakespeare wrote in *Hamlet*, 'Ay, there's the rub.'"

In 1988, Stephen Lekson published an intentionally provocative (as usual) historical and sociopolitical essay in which he argued (p. 214) that "Pueblo I Proto-kivas, Pueblo II kivas, and Pueblo III kivas are probably *not* really kivas in any meaningful functional sense, but are, instead, domestic pit structures." This is what Windes objected to in his 2010 email. Presumably, he still objects. Furthermore, in my opinion, the sociopolitical portions of Lekson's essay—focusing on attempts to eliminate or assimilate Pueblo peoples and to take their lands—although somewhat less developed, are *at least* as interesting as Lekson's architectural discussion. However, they are tangential to the Pepper–Wetherill and other unpublished records that are the focus here.

Lekson (1988, 222) references Hewett's (1938, 17–18) concept of the kiva:

> The structural gem of every house group was the kiva, the ceremonial chamber that is found in all the community house of the Rio Grande and San Juan valleys.
>
> This was the sanctuary—the place set aside, before the first stone of the dwelling was laid, for prayer and religious rites. No other object in Southwest archaeology is of greater interest than these subterranean sanctuaries.

Lekson then notes (222) that "Southwestern archaeology's concept of the kiva is *still* that of Hewett and the earliest anthropologists." Curiously, Hewett had not recognized an obvious flaw in his concept—that the "G Kivas" of Chetro Ketl (Miller 1937), among other examples, were up in a tower and *not* subterranean.

Lekson further states:

> For example, consider Anasazi ceremonial centers: if Pueblo III "kivas" are only by fiat and not by fact, then many "kivas" may not indicate much ceremony. But the effect of the received idea is far more pervasive than this simple and obvious example. The idea of the kiva underlies our conception of the pit house–pueblo transition, a key watershed in Southwestern prehistory (222).

Next Lekson (223–28) reviews alternative views of pit houses and kivas and notes (224): "'Kiva' is as ill-defined ethnographically as it is archaeologically." He then argues: "Considering pit structures simply as a class of structures, the Pueblo III kiva was a Basketmaker III pit house with several centuries of additions and alterations . . . Depending on one's perception, this record of continuity and change can be seen as a prolongation of the pit house, or as a foreshadowing of the ethnographic kiva" (228).

Lekson concludes his excellent provocative and speculative essay by stating (230):

In my opinion, pit structures, be they earth-walled or stone-walled, with or without benches and mealing bins, having or lacking sipapus and other esoteric window dressing, continued as a primary element of Anasazi residence until the A.D. 1300s—*four centuries* after the scenarios presented in almost every reconstruction of the pit house-to-pueblo transition. If the focus of interest is the loss of the pit house in Anasazi domestic building, I suggest the appropriate time period is *not* the A.D. 700s or the A.D. 900s, but the A.D. 1200s and the A.D. 1300s. If the focus of interest is the prehistoric analogues of modern Pueblo ceremonial structures[,] I suggest looking not at pit houses but at great kivas. From this perspective, the "origin" of Pueblo ceremonial architecture is completely separate from the pit house-to-pueblo argument. And if the focus of interest is the pit house-to-pueblo transition, I suggest rethinking the question, because that "transition" probably lasted 800 years.

I would make several comments: First, the Chacoan great houses, with the possible exception of Wijiji, which seems to have been built as a unit without significant changes or remodeling, were built, rebuilt, and further modified over periods of time, often hundreds of years. I have not attempted to do so, but I would imagine that dating a specific room or even a specific series of rooms would be difficult because of the reuse of timbers, overlapping masonry styles, and other factors (but see Windes and Ford 1996, who make the specific ins and outs of this architectural complexity much clearer). To get a bit ahead of myself and to preview part of the next section—"Burials"—Plog and Heitman (2010) suggest that, on the basis of radiocarbon dates, Pueblo Bonito burial rooms were possibly used over a three-hundred to four-hundred-year period, while Akins (2004) suggests a use period of about one hundred and seventy-five years based on pottery—the ceramic styles found with the burials.

Furthermore, as indicated in endnote 8 of the previous chapter, I prefer the term Great Sanctuary to Great Kiva because, following the ideas of my mentor, J. Charles Kelley, I think Great Sanctuaries were much more than enlarged kivas: they have a greater number of and more complex features, such as numerous and sealed wall niches (sometimes filled with rich and elaborate artifacts), raised masonry structures such as large firepits and possible foot drums, passageways that connect to adjoining rooms, and more (see Vivian and Reiter 1960). Moreover, where great houses have multiple kivas, they usually only have a *maximum* of two to three Great Sanctuaries (and Una Vida, for example, may have had only one). This indicates that Great Sanctuaries were community-wide ceremonial structures, whereas kivas were clan, society, or specific ritual ceremonial structures. We even find "isolated" Great Sanctuaries such as Casa Rinconada and Kin Nahasbas.

To return to Lekson (1988, 228): "If the focus of interest is the prehistoric analogues of modern Pueblo ceremonial structures[,] I suggest looking not at pit houses but at great kivas." I would argue that one might more properly look at modern Pueblo plazas, as the following illustrates. Several years ago, I was staying at a Pueblo village in the days prior to a major, multiday ceremony in order to distribute wild turkey, macaw, and parrot feathers from my Feather Distribution Project (Reyman 2008, 2023). On the first day of the ceremony, my host family, whose house adjoined one of several small plazas, erected a number of structures in the plaza, removing the components from a storage area of their home. Once completed, *katsinam* (I prefer the Hopi term to kachina) and accompanying religious officials entered the plaza and performed a series of rituals within its confines and at the structures. A large number of Pueblo people were in attendance, and I was privileged to see the entire ceremony. Upon completion of the ritual, the participants left first, followed by the Pueblo people. Once everyone was gone, my host family "deconstructed" what they had erected, filled in several small pits, and swept the plaza clean of all traces of the ceremony. They returned the components to storage in their home. A visitor would never know that this small empty plaza had, only a short time earlier, been the site of an important ritual with multiple participants and many village spectators. I watched this closely on several other occasions, and in two other Pueblos where I was staying during feather distributions. Plazas have superseded and replaced great kivas in modern Pueblos. I know of no Great Sanctuary, per se, in any modern Pueblo village.

In a July 2022 email, Lekson wrote to me:

In an old and questionable convention, each hearth is assumed to represent a family; thus [the] number of hearths equals the number of families, for which a numerical figure can be assigned. There are obvious problems with this convention ... Decades ago, I proposed a solution to this problem that recognizes that the round rooms conventionally called "kivas" are in fact pit-houses; thus the number of so-called "kivas" provide[s] a fair approximation for the number of households. That approach convinced archaeologists in the 1980s and 1990s, but with the passage of time, the field has slipped back to "kivas" being ceremonial structures ... This is unfortunate, and in assessing scholarship in Southwestern archaeology, the issue of "kivas" is, for me, in evaluating archaeological arguments. I cannot accept arguments that assume all the small round rooms at Chaco and Mesa Verde and elsewhere were something like modern "kivas," and not primarily residential.

Lekson (1988) makes a strong and interesting argument, but one I do not fully embrace, if only because of what I know from the ethnographic context. Kivas *are* sometimes residential units—almost full-time—for boys and young men, who go home only to eat and interact with family members, then return to the kiva to sleep and learn ritual. They are also part-time residential units for men while they are involved in ceremonies and used in weaving ceremonial garments. Among today's Pueblos, kivas have fire pits for heat and ceremonies or Franklin stoves for heat, and sometimes both. Kivas are entered through the roof via a ladder, or through a door in a wall, or both, depending upon one's status within the Pueblo. I've been allowed the privilege of both types of entries, again because of the Feather Distribution Project.

In short, I don't think of kivas as an either/or concept, i.e., residential units *or* ceremonial chambers. At least on the basis of historic and today's Pueblo usage, they are *both* residential and ceremonial structures. Whether this dual purpose extends back to ancient times, I can't say, but my best guess is to consider ancient Chacoan kivas both as residential units and as ceremonial structures, depending upon the context at the time. And if this makes me anachronistic as per Lekson's comment, I'm okay with that.

CHAPTER THREE

Pueblo Bonito Burials

I previously discussed the apparent paucity of burials at Chaco Canyon (Reyman 1989, 49–52). One point of this volume, as will become clear later, is that, as with firepits, what is apparent is neither real nor true; there were many more burials than are reported in the literature. Furthermore, it is worth reiterating that although Pepper was puzzled about the location of the burials from Pueblo Bonito itself, he found no general paucity of burials: "An extensive cemetery has been found west of and near Pueblo Pintado . . . Similar conditions should obtain in the case of Bonito and the other large pueblos of the Chaco Cañon" (Pepper 1920, 376). An anonymous reviewer (September 2007) of an earlier version of a manuscript, parts of which are included in this volume, commented:

> The extensive cemetery . . . west of and near Pueblo Pintado almost certainly was a reference to the numerous trash mounds associated with multiple small houses covering a large area west of Pueblo Pintado. That burials were removed from these sites is attested by the current presence of many large sandstone slabs that customarily covered burials from small house sites.

While it is true that slabs covered or lined the graves of such burials, that they did so does not mean these burials were in trash mounds and not burial mounds. This distinction receives further consideration below. Pepper's unpublished field notes and diary (Pepper 1896a, 1896b, 1899a) and Richard Wetherill's (1896) unpublished field notes describe in detail numerous burial mounds and their contents, and there are photographs of mounds, burials, and grave goods to accompany the written descriptions. Indeed, both men's unpublished notes specifically discuss slab-lined burials in mounds. Figure A.1 in Appendix A of the current volume shows one of these slab-lined burials in Mound 5 (figure 7) near Pueblo del Arroyo.

Pepper and Wetherill excavated dozens of burials from mounds west-southwest and west of Pueblo del Arroyo and also near to Bc-50 and Bc-51 (Pepper 1896b, Wetherill 1896). Their notes and photographs (see chapter 4, below) also make it clear that these were burial mounds and *not*

FIGURE 7. 1896 Pepper–Wetherill photograph of Mound 5, west-southwest of Pueblo del Arroyo. The arrow points to Mound 5, which has since fallen into the arroyo due to erosion, an example of which is seen in Bryan 1954, plate 5.

---

trash mounds for the Hosta Butte Phase pueblos. At one point, Wetherill labeled a small house site on the south side of the Chaco arroyo as "Burial Mound #5," but then noted during excavation that it was, in fact, a house site and not a burial mound (Wetherill 1896). It may have contained one or more burials, a not-unusual situation; in fact, the large burial mound west-southwest of Pueblo del Arroyo was later given the designation Burial Mound 5. Elsewhere in their notes, Pepper and Wetherill make it clear that they are digging burial mounds, not house sites or trash mounds. For example: "On the extreme right is the mound in which the skeletons were found, and near it the small ruin of the house in which the people probably lived" (Pepper 1899). These researchers knew the differences between burial mounds, house mounds, and trash mounds, and they knew where to find burial mounds, as their unpublished notes and extant photographs demonstrate. Wetherill's widow Marietta's unpublished but well-known interview and accompanying photograph add further support to the existence of burial mounds. Vivian (1948, 3; see also figure A.2 in the first appendix to this volume) states:

> Mrs. Wetherill gave me some photographs and I intended to bring them out here and give them to Charlie [Steen] when he came by. I forgot them and they're still in town. One of these shows a couple of burials out in a flat somewhere. There are no landmarks to identify it. Beside the burials are 4 or 5 pots. The burials are obviously very shallow—6 in. to a foot. [figure A.2]
>
> On the back of the photo she has written something like this[:] "This is a burial mound near Pueblo Bonito. There are lots of these mounds and most of them are about 20 feet high. The wind has blown all the sand and ashes off the cones and there are bones and skulls and pottery all over the mounds. Some of these are very large and *acres* in extent."[2]

It should be clear that, in the case of small house mounds, burials would not be near the top such that they could be uncovered by wind. They would be beneath house floors or well within the midden. Furthermore, small house mounds are not twenty to thirty feet high. (I assume the accuracy of Marietta Wetherill's account, but I could be wrong.) That the skeletal materials were apparently on top of ashes is consistent with a burial mound and not interment in a house mound or trash midden. The graves, if you will, seem to have been prepared.

In another example, Richard Wetherill (1896) reports that in one mound they uncovered at least ten burials in a one-meter-by-three-meter trench. That's a densely packed group of burials, unlike what would be found in a small house mound or trash midden. In another, much larger mound east-southeast of Pueblo del Arroyo (Mound 5—figure 7)—so large that sixty-four eight-foot-square grids did not cover its entirety[3]— Wetherill states that in a single trench they uncovered forty skeletons, again a densely packed situation, unlike what would be found in a house mound or trash midden. I examined aerial photographs at the Southwest

Cultural Resource Center at the University of New Mexico in the summer of 1982 and found that the outline of Pepper's excavation units seemed to be still faintly visible for what might have been the remaining portion of the mound, though the mound itself no longer seemed intact. LiDAR mapping was not available to me then but would be useful now as a check, if it covers this specific area.

Questions arise pertaining to these burials. Among them: Why were they not reported in Pepper's various publications? This question is of particular interest because in *Pueblo Bonito* (Pepper 1920) he did report on the excavation of burials from other mounds at Chaco Canyon (26–27, 339–51) and publish a photograph of Skeleton 20 from Mound 2 (348, figure 154). He also wrote with regard to Mounds 1 and 2 on the south side of the canyon: "Two of these mounds were mapped and all of the burials in them photographed and the specimens removed" (26). But where are the remains of the thirty or thirty-one individuals uncovered, and where are the accompanying grave goods? And why were the mounds not completely excavated?[4]

These questions are difficult to answer, especially after more than a century has passed, but the following answers can be suggested on the basis of the unpublished field notes and published data for other mound excavations. Most burials and accompanying grave goods from this site seem not to have been reported. Pepper and Wetherill uncovered and apparently removed the materials (Pepper 1920, 26), but did not ultimately preserve or keep all of them. Some objects are at the American Museum of Natural History and the Field Museum and are marked with the "H" designation indicating the Hyde Exploring Expedition. They did report that many of the skeletons were in poor condition (Pepper 1896b; Wetherill 1896; cf. Pepper 1920, 339), e.g., "The body had completely wasted away so that the position of the grave could not be ascertained" (Pepper 1920, 250). It might also be the case that Pepper's reference to removing "specimens" does *not* refer to skeletal remains but only to grave goods. Moreover, because the catalogue of numbered items from the Hyde Exploring Expedition does not always specify provenience, it is difficult to be certain which, if any, of the ceramics and other objects came from Mounds 1 and 2 and which from other sites and burial mounds. Therefore, it is possible that many, perhaps most skeletal remains from these two mounds were either left in situ or discarded along with grave goods that were also in poor condition, not an unusual practice at the time. It is also possible that Wetherill sold some of the better-preserved skeletal materials, pottery, and other funerary objects to museums and collectors, another customary practice of that time and one in which he and his brothers regularly engaged with collections they made from Mesa Verde, Grand Gulch, and elsewhere. Wetherill sold a collection to the Field Museum, and a number of his collections were displayed at both the 1893 World's Columbian Exposition in Chicago and the 1904 Louisiana Purchase Exposition in St. Louis.

In summary, some of the skeletal materials and grave goods were left in the ground and could still be there. Some were discarded and have since been destroyed: it was customary practice beyond Judd's time to dump discarded materials and back dirt into the arroyo. Some are scattered throughout museums and perhaps private collections in the United States and in other countries. This is certainly the case for some of the Chacoan materials at the Field Museum of Natural History (Dorsey 1904; Wetherill 1904, 1905).

Finally, the last question—Why were the mounds not completely excavated?—is the easiest to answer because Wetherill (1896, 19) tells us in his unpublished field notes that during the excavation of a mound on the south side of the canyon, they found many burials, but uncovered so few "unusual" pots that they lost interest, quit excavating, and went on to another mound, where they encountered the same situation. Perhaps the absence of significant grave goods, especially in comparison to objects found with burials in Pueblo Bonito, led Pepper and Wetherill to conclude that the individuals buried in the mounds were not persons of importance (Stephen Plog, personal communication 2003). Pepper (1920, 347) wrote essentially the same thing in *Pueblo Bonito* with regard to Mound 2 on the south side of the canyon, although this work was done *before* the excavation of Pueblo Bonito Rooms 32–33: "Skeletons 13, 14, 15 [in Mound 2] were unproductive and as there was no evidence of other remains, which we ascertained by sounding in various places, I concluded to stop operations in this part of the mound."

A final note regarding these mounds: numbering began with the 1896 excavations. However, Pepper's and Wetherill's unpublished field notes from 1897–1901 *seem* to indicate that they *may* have, in some cases, numbered the burial mounds again starting with #1 for the specific year, which would be confusing. The only way to sort this out is through the descriptions of the mounds' locations. But given that the mounds on the south side of the canyon are relatively close together, this decipherment is not always certain. Their mound numbering system is an unresolved problem.

Nevertheless, to the extent that the revised population estimates are based on the *apparent* paucity of burials, as with the issue of the number of hearths, these estimates must certainly be revised again, and substantially *upward*. The *apparent* paucity of burials is just that—apparent—and not as real as supposed.

Pueblo Bonito Rooms 32–33

The contents of Rooms 32–33 at Pueblo Bonito constitute one of the richest assemblages of archaeological mortuary materials found anywhere in the Southwest: fourteen burials accompanied by thousands of turquoise, shell, wood, basketry, ceramic, and other artifacts, including wooden flutes and a board decorated in an invested paint technique. Pepper (1909, 1920, 129–79) described the contents of Rooms 32 and 33 in some detail; indeed, Pepper (1920, 163) wrote that "A full account of its contents [Room 33] has been published in 'The Exploration of a Burial-Room in Pueblo Bonito, New Mexico'" (Pepper 1909), but, as will become clear, as with *Pueblo Bonito* (Pepper 1920), it is not a full account. Among the important materials he omitted from both publications are his drawings of the stratigraphic profile for Room 32 (figure 8) and the burials in Room 33 (figures 9–15); see also Reyman 1989, 45–52. Pepper also omitted almost everything about the condition of the room and the conditions under which he excavated, which are included in the lengthy quotation later in this chapter from his 1899 lecture notes.

I have discussed these drawings and other information previously (e.g., Reyman 1971, 1978a, 1989) and will not repeat those discussions here except to note that any consideration of Rooms 32–33 must also consider the materials found in adjacent and nearby rooms: 28, 28a, 51, 53,

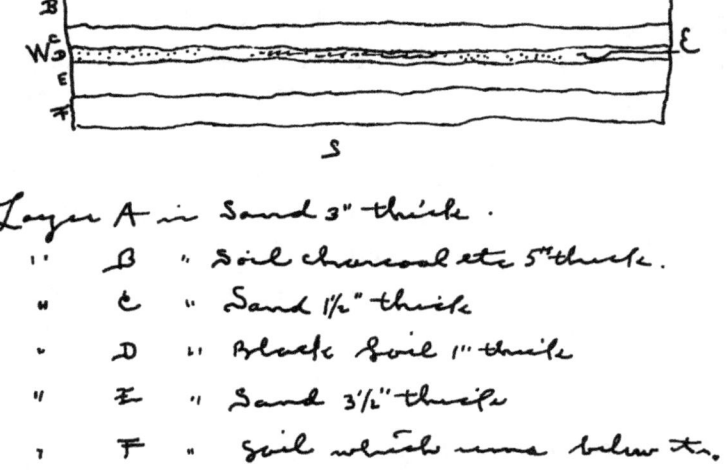

FIGURE 8. Pepper's 1896 drawing of and notes on the stratigraphy in Room 32, Pueblo Bonito.

FIGURE 9

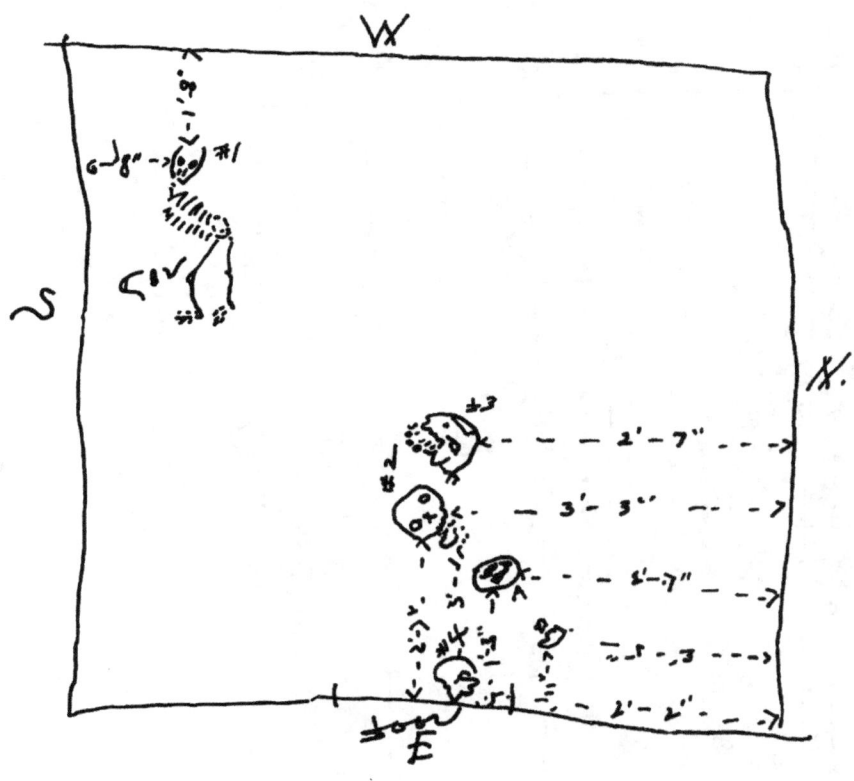

FIGURES 9–15. Pepper's 1896 field drawings of the skeletal materials in Rooms 32–33, Pueblo Bonito.

FIGURE 10

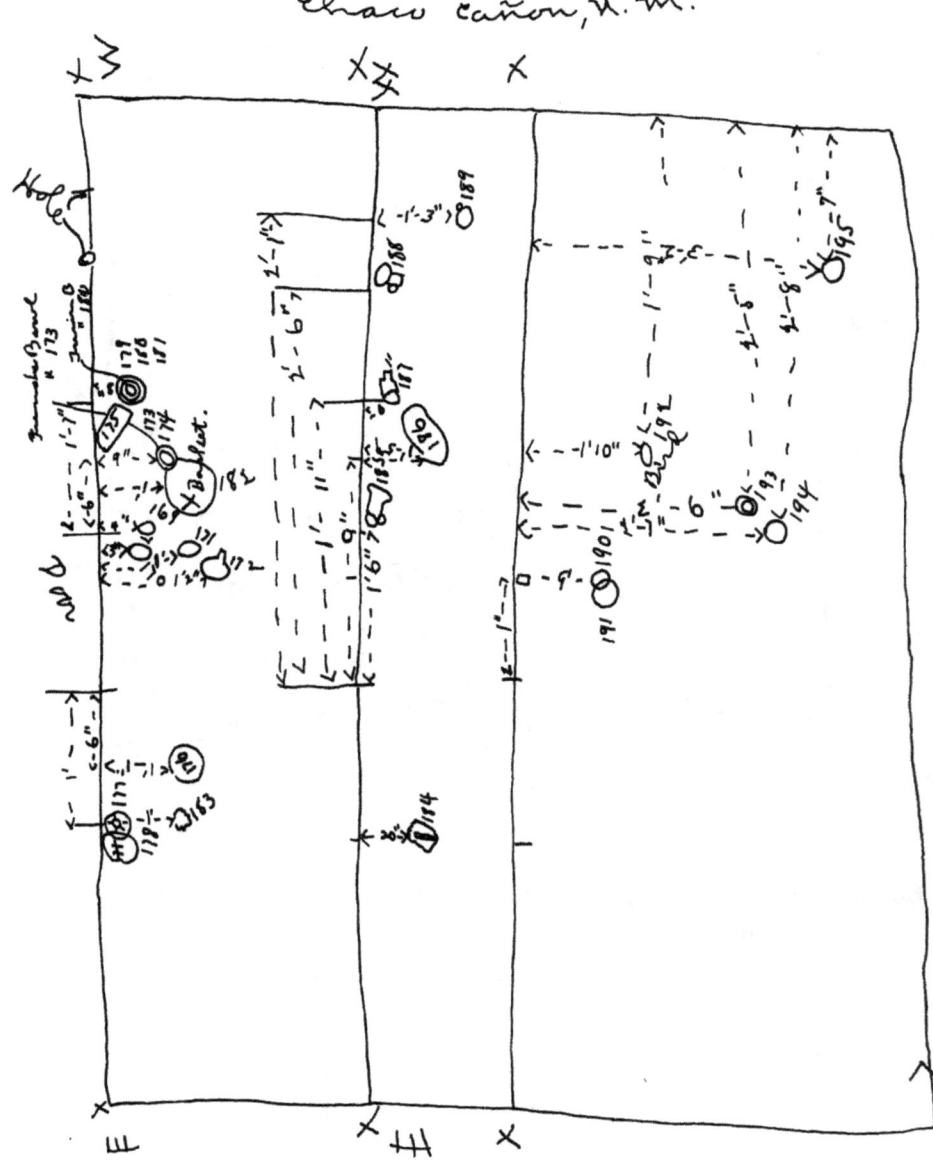

FIGURE 11

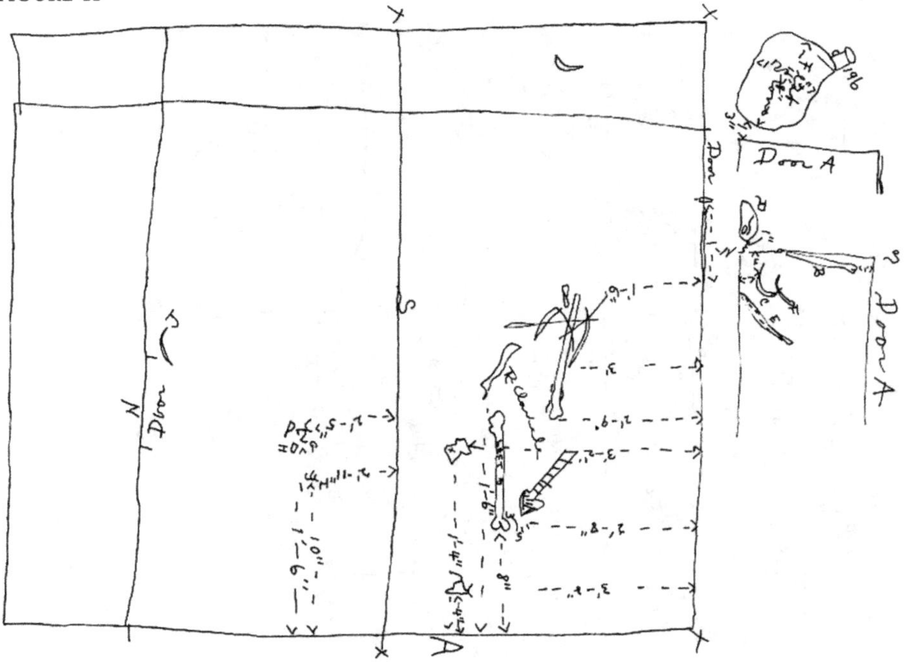

FIGURE 12

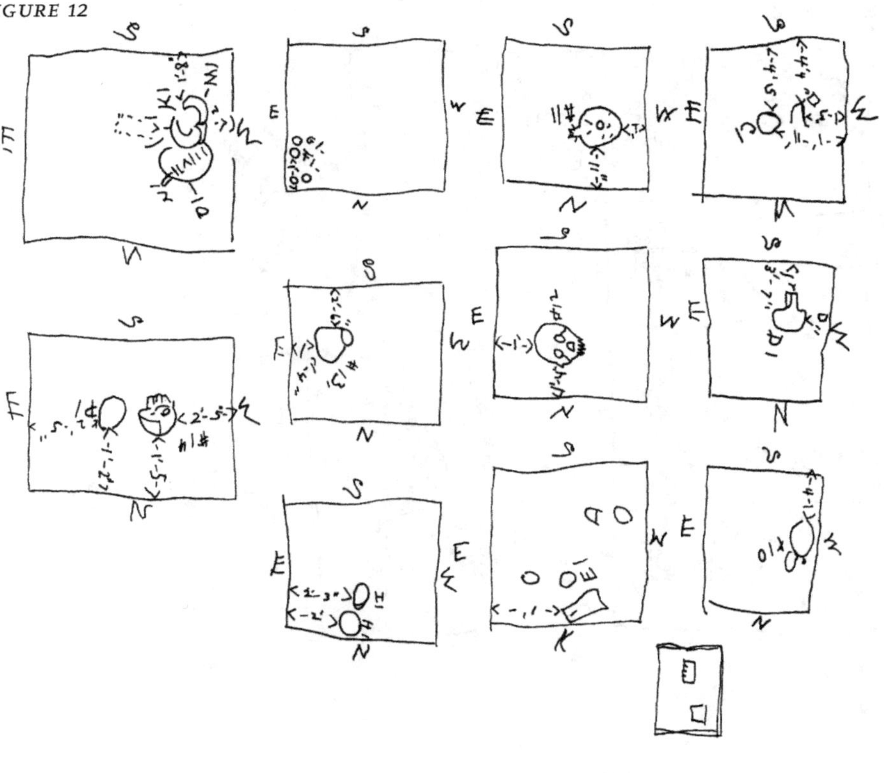

FIGURE 13

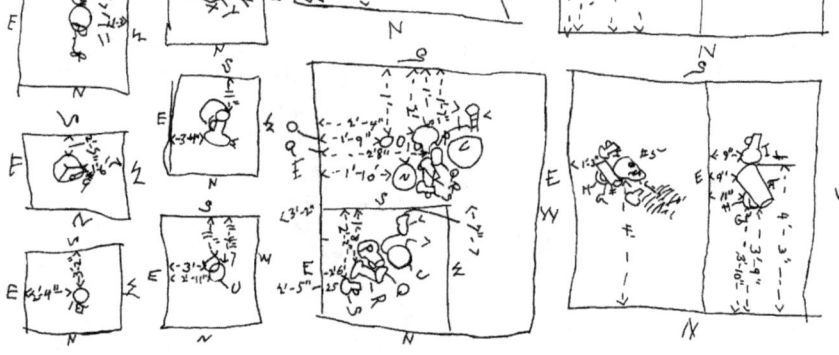

FIGURE 14

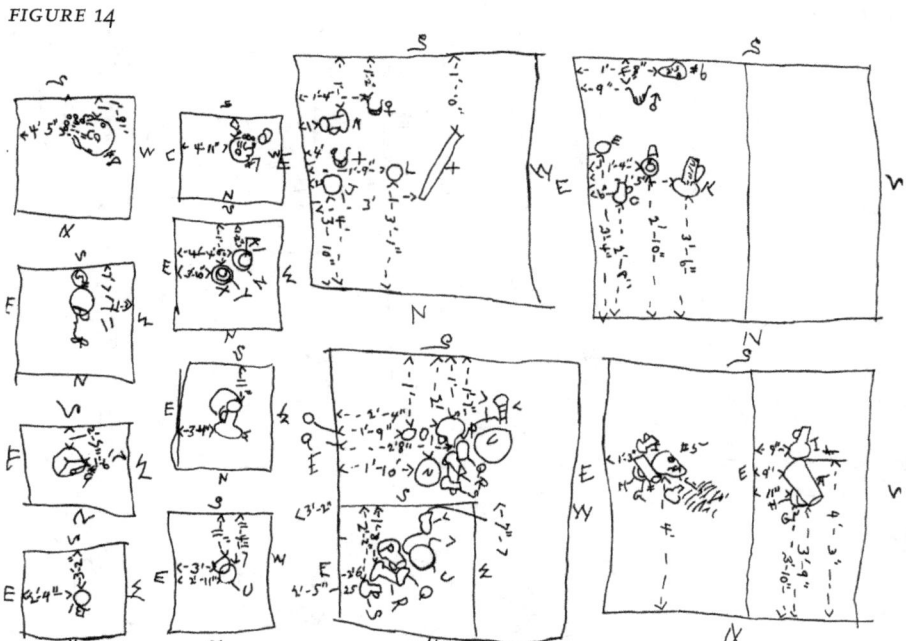

FIGURE 15

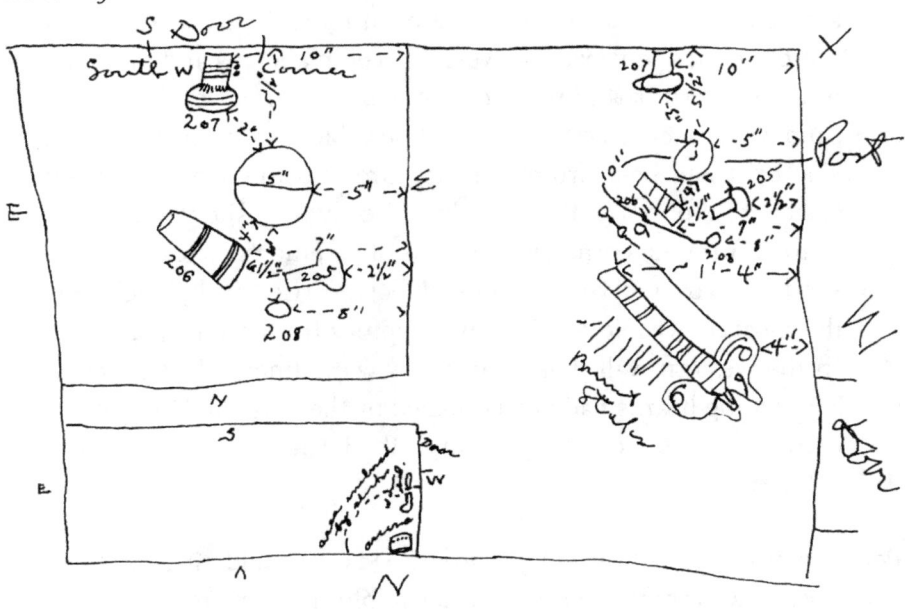

and 56 (Reyman 1978a, 252; Reyman 1982). Both the architectural and cultural contexts indicate that these rooms, located in the oldest section of Pueblo Bonito, apparently functioned as a ceremonial and mortuary complex.

Pepper's unpublished field notes, diary entries, and other documents add greatly to our understanding of this complex. They also provide a rich context for his actual working conditions, context that is absent from Pepper's 1909, 1920, and other published reports. By contrast, his published descriptions of the physical conditions in the rooms and the conditions under which he worked are notable for their lack of contextual detail, a lack of specific information that led to a serious misunderstanding by me of the effects of these conditions on the contents of Rooms 32–33. For example, Pepper (1920, 129) described the beginning of the work in Room 32 as follows:

> With the removal of the stones with which the doorway in the north wall of Room 28 was closed, a wall of drifted sand was

encountered. Owing to the presence of an opening west of, and a little above this doorway, it had been possible to ascertain that there was an open space between the ceiling beams and the sand, in the western part of the room. When the surface of the drifted sand was reached, a candle made it possible to examine the room. The drift had been from the eastward and the sand was piled almost to the roof at that end, but directly opposite the doorway in the northwest corner, was a mass of ceremonial sticks . . . The sand was covered with various objects, carried in by pack rats, the most noticeable of which were spines from cactus plants . . . In the western wall there was a doorway, almost filled by sand. The ceiling beams had been crushed by the mass of débris above them, and in the central portion of the beams were cracked and splintered.

Pepper's discussion of the entry to Room 33 is almost identical in both his 1909 and 1920 reports, and the earlier publication is cited here: "Room 33 is directly west of and connected with Room 32 . . . The room proved somewhat smaller than Room 32; but the sand had not filled it so deeply as the other room" (Pepper 1909, 197).

In describing the skeletal remains found in Room 33, Pepper noted that the skulls, mandibles, and other bones were generally disarticulated. He explains this situation as follows:

In considering the contents of this room, it must be remembered that the greater part of the material had been affected from time to time by streams of water that no doubt poured through the eastern doorway after each heavy shower. The swirling water displaced the parts of the skeletons to so great an extent that, of the fourteen skeletons unearthed in this room, only two (Nos. 13, 14) remained *in situ* [fully articulated]; in most cases the under jaw [mandible] had been detached and was found some distance from the skull. With the two skeletons just mentioned was found a mass of material that will be described as having been found *in situ*.

The other objects from the room—with the exception of the skulls, the pottery vessels, and some of the turquoise objects—will be treated in a general way, as it was impossible to determine with which skeletons the various pieces had been buried (Pepper 1909, 209–10).

When I first read and reflected upon Pepper's descriptions of Rooms 32 and 33 and their contents, I was skeptical that water had caused so much disarticulation of the skeletal remains and "jumbling" of the accompanying artifacts. Pepper did not publish photographs of this skeletal material, so I had no visual data to examine. Nevertheless, it seemed at the time that there was another possible explanation for the situation that he encountered:

> Having examined Pepper's notes and photographs at the American Museum of Natural History [in winter 1970–1971], I am less certain than he about the presumed effects of water on the deposits. Although the rotted condition of some of the wood artifacts indicates that the room fill, at one time, was moist, the excellent condition of much of the wood and other perishables and the *lack* of disturbance among many other artifacts, especially small items like shell and turquoise beads (e.g., Pepper 1909, 221), suggest that the disturbing effects of water were not as serious as Pepper believed (Reyman 1978a: 253–254) . . . Given that many of the artifactual materials show *no* effects of water disturbance, it is reasonable to suggest another explanation for the disarticulated state of these skeletons. These facts, plus the consistent detachment of the skull or mandible from the rest of the body and the crushed condition or "unnatural position" (Pepper 1909, 219) of several skulls, suggest *deliberate* disarticulation [decapitation] (Reyman 1978a, 255).

In 1980 a colleague and physical anthropologist, Martin Nickels, collaborated with me at the American Museum of Natural History as we examined the skeletal remains from Rooms 32 and 33. He concluded there was *no* evidence for decapitation. In 1984, I obtained access to and read Pepper's unpublished diaries, room notes, and other materials (Pepper

1896a, 1896b, 1899). These records make the context of Rooms 32 and 33 much clearer for the time Pepper worked in them, including the likelihood that some disturbance to the room contents was probably due to the difficult working conditions there, among which were torrents of water from thunderstorms that coursed through the rooms from time to time.

The following lengthy description is from Pepper's (1899b) notes for a lecture he planned to deliver at the American Museum of Natural History. There are three different versions, each with alterations, some of which Pepper included within brackets, presumably allowing him to make changes depending upon his audience. These bracketed alternatives are retained in the version cited below to give the reader a better sense of Pepper's style, and I have also put them in italics to make them stand out more clearly, most notably one exceptionally long alternate section toward the end. I use double brackets [[ ]] within the italics to indicate where Pepper included additional alternate wordings. I do not know which version he delivered, or if, indeed, he delivered any one of the three versions as written. The information provided, however, markedly changes our understanding of the physical conditions in Rooms 32–33:

> In the western wall [*of room 32*] there was a doorway, partly open; true the space was small, for the sand was piled to within ten inches of the lintel—I endeavored to get a glimpse of the interior of the next room, by means of the candle that I carried, but its faint rays revealed nothing but a sea of [*stygian*] darkness—it was really painful [*maddening*] to think of the possibilities of that chamber and not to be able to see it—it was a temptation that one [*I*] could not resist: there was a fascination that could not be overcome, so throwing myself face downward upon the sand I glided backward with a snake-like movement, through the door—the sand, instead of being soft and yielding, seemed like a bed of stinging nettles, for it was filled with those terrible [*cactus*] spines [*and my plight would have put to shame some of the heathenish rites of the Penitentes*]—but I kept on and my body slowly disappeared in the [*yawning*] mouth of—I knew not what—at last I was suspended in mid-air with only my arms and head in the room that I was about to leave [*32*]—I braced myself for the fall: I knew not

how far it would be: it might be but a few feet, again it could be a score—then there was the cheering thought that there might be rattlesnakes, centipedes, or scorpions, to receive me [*as their rightful prey—but I would not retreat so*] but I gave the final push, and as I passed through the opening, the space was so narrow that I had to fold my sombrero over my face to keep from coming in contact with the sand—the fall was but trifling and I immediately lighted the candle and looked about me: near my head there was a bunch of ceremonial sticks which protruded from the space beneath the ceiling beams—two flutes were lying in the sand in one corner, there was a burial-mat in the opposite one, and both of the others had their quota of ceremonial sticks. So much for general appearances, which are pleasing—the work was another proposition—it was, to say the least, trying. The first investigations were made with a trowel, and I had not been working a quarter of an hour ere I found a portion of a human skeleton, which was the first evidence of the fourteen bodies that had been laid away in this box-like room, when Bonito was the scene of life and activity. The room was six [*eight*] feet square and contained four feet of sand—in this scant deposit, fourteen bodies had been buried—not in the deposit, really, as they were part of it, for, removing the remains and their wrappings would have materially reduced the thickness of the mass. Just think of a deposit only eight feet square and four feet thick, and then endeavor to realize what part of it was once the clay that surrounded the skeletons that were lying beneath the surface. [*Faint hearted people beware: field work, in some of its phases is apt to be too realistic.*] In this room I worked for three weeks, carefully uncovering each object of interest and making accurate measurements ere it was removed, and this too in a place where the dust was so thick at times, that the light of the candles about the room, could hardly be seen—at seven in the morning I would enter the room and work until noon, then from two until six. [*but I paid for it in those few weeks I was reduced from a strong healthy man to a mere shadow—I lost over twenty five pounds, and was tired and sick when the work was completed*] to show what stifling mummy-dust will do, let me site [sic] the case of a gentleman who was with me: he went into the room and stayed for only half an hour but when night came he [*tossed and rolled upon his bed*] had a burning fever: why I was not affected in a like manner I cannot say, unless it was due to my strong constitution. This room was fifteen feet below the surface—to reach it one had to pass from the room where the mass of pottery was found [[Room 28]], through a doorway only two feet wide, thence through an underground room and through a second doorway— there was absolutely no ventilation and the clouds of dust that were stirred up, had no alternative, but must settle again, at least as much of it as was not drawn into the lungs—for two whole days I occupied this room, uncovering skulls and skeletons, while the men were at work two miles up the canon—it was pleasant work, indeed, with beams in the outer room creaking from the enormous weight above them and threatening to let down at any moment[5] [*and leave one to a death by suffocation.*] one of these days I remember particularly—I was searching for the pottery and turquoise ornaments, which were buried with most of the bodies: my face was within six inches of the earth, as the candle light was very dim. I had just found a slab of turquoise and was bending forward, eagerly searching the sand for more, when a piece of matting obstructed my view: it was but a fragment so I tore it up, and there [*with grinning jaws and gaping eye sockets*] lay a skull: the mouth was open and the shining teeth gave it a look of fiendish enjoyment, as though it fully appreciated the joke.

Had I not been hardened to such sights, it might have startled me, as it was, I simply [*raised my head and said, in the words of Shakespeare, "Alas poor Yoric* [sic]*"* then covered it up to wait its turn. But human nature has its limit of endurance: in my eagerness I failed to realize it: one morning, when I had been at work for over an hour, the room grew suddenly cold, [*ice-laden breezes seemed to seep through the doorway where I knew no air was stirring—I tried to overcome the feeling, for it was a horrible sensation in such a* [[*that uncanny*]]—*place, but I could not—a cold perspiration oozed from the pores and caused me to almost shiver—my head began to swim, but with an effort I controlled myself and commenced* to work again, hoping that the trouble would abate, but it returned with renewed force—then came the thought that I was alone and no help was near—everything was swimming before me, but I managed to crawl through the doorway into the next room, and then to the fresh air—this seemed to dispel the vertigo and in a short time I was able to walk to camp get [[some]] medicine—I did not return that day, but the next morning I commenced again—I was weak and really not able to cope with the [[nauseating]] finds that were to greet me—the dust dimmed the lights and dimmed my vision, choking me at one moment and filling my lungs the next] and I was overcome with a nausea and vertigo that compelled me to desist, but the next day the work was resumed, and, though I was quite weak, it was carried on until all the specimens had been removed. Then a stratum was reached where the water had penetrated and converted the textiles and mats into a soggy mass—the odors emanating from this foetid [sic] deposit would suffice to test the enthusiasm of any scientist, but, as though this were not enough, unsightly worms appeared to make it still more unpleasant—such conditions would be looked upon with disfavor on the surface, but in such a room—well all things must come to an end, and in this case it was the work instead of the worker.

We started for civilization soon after completing the operations [work] in this room, and, though I had suffered physically in the prosecution of the researches, I carried with me a collection of turquoise ornaments that will gladden the eyes of many an enthusiast and which I hope all of you may see at no far distant day.

In places, Pepper's account reads like the purple prose for which the adventurer Richard Halliburton became famous some three decades later. Pepper's unpublished notes, in contrast to his later published reports, make it clear that as he dug down into the room fill, the conditions changed from dusty to waterlogged. In retrospect, it is now understandable and seems somewhat more likely that the amount of water that coursed through the room was possibly sufficient to disarticulate at least some of the skeletal remains and certainly was sufficient to scatter turquoise and other small objects in the deposits. This also explains, at least in part, the absence of the textiles and mats noted by Pepper as having been found in Room 33 in the extant collections from Pueblo Bonito in the American Museum of Natural History and that were formerly in the Museum of the American Indian, Heye Foundation (and presumably have been mostly transferred to the National Museum of the American Indian). These woven materials were either so rotted or decayed that they were not kept, or they did not survive the drying-out process following excavation, as Pepper reports in his journal and lecture notes.

In a 2006 paper, Plog and Heitman question Pepper's argument that water disarticulated the skeletal remains. They state that "field drawings from his 1896 notebook . . . show intact stratigraphy in Room 32—the room through which water would need to have flowed to ever reach Room 33" (18). They note that the drawing depicts objects in place, undisturbed but also that "these provocative sources do not bring closure to a century of debate."

I agree that the debate is not closed. The stratigraphy does not appear to me as intact as Plog and Heitman view it and less so when one looks at other drawings plus notes and photographs from Rooms 32 and 33 (e.g., Reyman 1989, 46–47; see also figures 9–18, this volume). Furthermore, Pepper (1920, 140–43) discussed the decayed condition of ceremonial sticks in Room 32 as a result of "recent rains," and water could have entered Room 33 through the ceiling, as well as through Room 32, to create the "soggy mass" and waterlogged conditions described above.

Nevertheless, one inference all should be able to agree upon is that the materials from Rooms 32 and 33 were even *more* abundant—richer in number and variety—than reported in the published literature. A second inference to be drawn from Pepper's notes is that the twelve burials in Room 33 above the wood plank floor[6] (Pepper 1909), and perhaps the burial in Room 32, though only partial when Pepper unearthed it, were either laid on blankets or mats or wrapped in them, in a manner similar to burial practices described ethnographically for the Pueblos (see, e.g., Simmons 1942, 256–57, 313–15).

In 1989 I published Pepper's previously unpublished drawing of the stratigraphy he recorded and described for Room 32 (Pepper 1920, 137) and his similarly unpublished drawings of the skeletal remains and some of the accompanying artifacts for Room 33, along with some brief undated notes on implications of stratigraphic excavation (Reyman 1989, 45–48, figures 4–1 and 4–2). They are included in this volume in a larger format as figures 8–15. It's important to note that although Pepper was not consistent in his recording of stratigraphy for excavated rooms, mounds, and other features, the stratigraphy he did record put him a couple of decades ahead of his time in the Southwest. Nels Nelson (1914, 1916) is usually credited with the first stratigraphic excavations in the Southwest, but Pepper's work dates to 1896. Furthermore, Pepper effectively "piece plotted" the positions of the fourteen skulls in Rooms 32–33 and the objects found with the skeletal remains. These are documented in Pepper (1909) by categories such as "Measurements Indicating the Positions of the Skulls" (231–32) and "the respective positions of the specimens described, including the distance of each from the ceiling beams" (232–34). Again, Pepper was far ahead of others in Southwest archaeology in recording such positions and publishing his results, and there are more such data in his unpublished field notes.

Using these excavation data and Pepper's drawings, published papers, and unpublished notes as guides, I hired Julianne Snider, then a staff member of the Illinois State Museum, to collaborate with me in 1993 and commissioned her to create scale drawings of Rooms 32–33, the skeletal remains, and the rooms' contents. The results are published here as figures 16–18 and make it clear just how tightly packed with materials the rooms were and the complexity of the burial context.

Pepper's discussion of Rooms 32–33 focuses much more on the cultural contents and less on the skeletal remains. This is understandable because of the spectacular nature of the artifacts. He wrote a lengthy chapter on the contents of Room 33 for the *Putnam Anniversary Volume* (Pepper 1909) and discussed the room at some length on pages 163–77 of *Pueblo Bonito* (Pepper 1920). However, Pepper's unpublished notes and our examination of both the skeletal material and the artifacts add more significant information to the published record. Some of this is particularly relevant in terms of Southwest–Mesoamerican connections, especially in light of the twenty-first-century findings of cacao residue in Chacoan cylindrical vessels (Crown and Hurst 2009). The majority of these jars (111) were found in Room 28, with three in Room 32, 19 in Room 39b, and one or two each in eleven other rooms (Pepper 1920, 359–62, table 2). It is worth noting that Pepper believed they bore distinct resemblances to Cakchiquel Mayan jars (Pepper 1920, 121).[7] Other Mesoamerican and Mesoamerican-influenced objects from Rooms 32–33 include a shell trumpet (H/3653; *Strombus galeatus* Swainson) found with skeleton 14 in Room 33 (cf. Mills and Ferguson 2008), pseudo-cloisonné investment on a painted "design board" (H/4500; Pepper 1920, 156, 158–59) from Room 32 and on a painted flute (H/4563; Pepper 1909, 199–200, figures 2–3; Pepper 1920, 164, 166), a cylindrical basket completely covered with turquoise mosaic (H/12758; Pepper 1920, 164, 169), and pyrite sets possibly used to make a mirror (Pepper 1909, 245).[8]

One of the more interesting *foreign* objects found with skeleton 14 in Room 33 is shown in plate 2. Pepper (1909, 229–30, figure 4; see also Pepper 1920, figure 76c) described it as follows:

> An object having an animal form was found. This figure (R1-H 3657)[9] is made of a soft but very compact stone. The greater part is light pink color; but there is an area of chalky white on the underside, extending through to the tail. This latter part is so much disintegrated that the material rubs off at the slightest touch. This object in its entirety is 8.7 cm. in length, and 3.3 cm. in width at the widest part, that is, across the shoulders. It is 1.6 cm. in thickness at the shoulder, tapering from this point to the nose, also to the wedge-shaped tail. . . . The body is marked off from the head by a deep groove on each side. The head is beautifully carved. One feature is a shovel-like projection, evidently made to represent a flat nose. There are pits forming eyes which evidently were once inlaid with pieces of turquoise. A band of the same material passes across the neck. This object was obviously made to be used as a pendant. To prevent the cord from wearing away the exceptionally soft material, the makers inserted a bird bone in a hole drilled just above the neck; the opening on each side was countersunk, and the space filled with gum. Over each end a large turquoise bead was placed, one being in position when the object was found. These completely covered the ends of the bone, which otherwise would have detracted from the finish of the figure. Whether this object was made to represent a real or a mythical animal is not determined.

PLATE 2. The turquoise-inlaid shell bird figurine (R1/H3657, properly H10418) found with individual 14 in Room 33, Pueblo Bonito. *Photo*: Jonathan E. Reyman.

Pepper's description is accurate except for one critical point. When we examined the object, it seemed clear to us that the base material was shell, not stone—but what kind of shell? We took the object to Dr. Harold S. Feinberg, then Curator and Chair of the Department of Living Invertebrates at the American Museum of Natural History, who identified it a portion of the hinge from an exceptionally large bivalve (clam), probably from the east (?) coast of Florida. However, the hinge had been so modified when the object was created that Feinberg was unable to identify the species other than to note it is now probably extinct. Nevertheless, the presence of shell was evidence for at least one long-distance marine contact, indirect or direct, with the Southeast. As for identifying the animal represented, Nickels and I think it is an effigy of an unidentified species of bird with its wings folded against its body.

NEW, PREVIOUSLY UNPUBLISHED DATA FOR INDIVIDUALS 13 AND 14, ROOM 33

As noted earlier, I originally thought that the twelve above-floor burials in Room 33 were perhaps decapitated as sacrificial offerings to accompany the two individuals interred beneath the plank floor (Reyman 1978a, 255). As also noted, subsequent examination of the skeletal materials and Pepper's unpublished excavation records proved this not to be the case. However, examination of the skeletal remains and the same records yielded added information that Pepper had not published, had only barely hinted at, and from which he derived an incorrect conclusion. In short, both individuals buried beneath the plank floor had been deliberately killed—murdered[10] (cf. Akins and Schelberg 1984, 91; Marsden 2011, 196–203 and passim).

In both his earlier *Putnam Anniversary Volume* chapter "The Exploration of a Burial-Room in Pueblo Bonito, New Mexico" (Pepper 1909) and *Pueblo Bonito* (Pepper 1920, 163–77), Pepper spent considerable time discussing the materials found with the burials and especially with skeletons 13 and 14. But he said little about the skeletons themselves other than to note the positions of objects relative to them. Even here, however, he wrote that because of the disturbance in Room 33, "it was impossible to determine with which skeletons the various pieces had been buried"

(Pepper 1909, 209–10). For skeleton 13 he wrote only that "Under the floor, at a distance of 5 ft. 5 in. below the ceiling-beams, skull No. 13 was found resting on its right side. The body extended toward the southwest, and the bones were in place" (222). As is clear in Appendix A, plate A.1 of this book, however, there is a deep cut mark on the lower portion of the left parietal such as could have been made by a knife or other sharp blade. Pepper either never saw this or failed to recognize its significance and didn't mention it.

The next skeleton found (No. 14) was in situ. Pepper devoted much more space to it and its cranium (H/3672) than he did for the skeleton and cranium of individual 13 (H/3671). The head was in an upright position, and was 7 ft. 9 in. from the ceiling, about two feet lower in the deposit than skeleton 13. The face was turned toward the southeast, and the lower jaw was in place. The upper jaw was broken and had fallen apart. The right side of the cranium was crushed, and there were two holes and a gash in the frontal bone. The skeleton, which was intact, was extended about north and south. The arms extended along the sides of the body. The legs were spread and bent upward, the feet being close together and resting against the southern wall.

In view of the fact that the objects found with this body were in place, I will consider them before giving a general résumé of the specimens found with the other bodies. The skeleton itself was resting on a layer of wood ashes that had been spread on the leveled floor of yellow sand. From the general care bestowed upon this body, and from the character and quantity of the objects found with it, the deceased must have been a person of rank (Pepper 1909, 223).

Pepper described many of the grave goods and their positions relative to skeleton 14 and stated (225), "The presence of so many ornaments made of turquoise would itself seem sufficient evidence for concluding that this person had been of high rank." Pepper (1909, 1920) and Akins (2003) discuss in detail the materials accompanying skeleton 14, so there is no need to repeat the inventory except to note that it was the richest burial found at Chaco Canyon and one of the richest in the entire Southwest.

Appendix A, plates A.2 to A.4 show the two large puncture wounds, the gash to the frontal bone, and the total destruction of the facial area. This individual (H/3672) suffered massive head trauma; it was not just the right side of his cranium that was crushed, as stated by Pepper, but his entire facial area was bashed in. He may also have been scalped. Scalp societies were present among the post-contact Pueblos. What he had endured appeared to Nickels and me as clearly deliberate: he was murdered, which differs sharply from Pepper's conclusion that:

> Owing to the havoc wrought by the inflow of water, the only preparations for burial that could be noted were those in connection with skeletons Nos. 13 and 14. In this instance the floor had been covered with a layer of yellow sand on which a layer of wood-ashes had been placed. The bodies were placed near each other, and, from the positions in which they were found, it would seem that they had been buried at the same time. The skull of one of them was crushed,—a feature which suggests an *accident* in which the two persons, and perhaps the others buried with them, may have lost their lives (Pepper 1909, 248–49, emphasis mine).

In fact, none of the other skeletal materials bears evidence of premortem or perimortem trauma. Furthermore, to the contrary with regard to Pepper's statement, the deep cut mark on the skull of skeleton 13 and the extreme trauma to the skull of skeleton 14 and the cut marks on his left femur indicate deliberate killings—not the results of an accident but murder. It must also be noted that there is almost no evidence of trauma to the postcranial skeletons of both men except for the femur cuts on skeleton 14, which would seem to indicate that he had tried to ward off blows from the knife or spear blade that pierced his skull and the club that smashed in his face (cf. Akins and Schelberg 1984, 91; Akins 1986, 116–17; and Akins 2003, 97).

The significance of what happened to individual 13 and especially individual 14 is this: As Kennett et al. 2017 have demonstrated, *all of* the individuals in Rooms 32–33—a tomb setting—belonged to a single "elite" matriline, elite as indicated by their interment in the prepared tomb. Clearly this was an important group within Pueblo Bonito. But what occurred that at least one and almost certainly two of these elite individuals were murdered? Ultimately, their relatively high status was no deterrent to their final, fatal mistreatment.

Akins (1986, 114–17) discusses Room 33, the skeletal materials, and the rich assemblage of materials ("an incredible amount of ornamentation") in some detail. She makes no mention of the cut mark on H/3671, but with respect to H/3672 and skeleton 14 she writes:

> Pepper also noted that Number 14 had two holes and a gash in the frontal bone; these indeed appear to be green [i.e., greenstick] bone fractures. Number 14 also has what appear to be chops along the left parietal and temporal juncture, a gash to the right parietal, and cuts or chops on the left femur, suggesting that he died in a confrontation of some sort (Akins 1986, 116–17).

Although Akins and Schelberg (1984, 91) wrote earlier that the evidence suggested the men suffered "violent deaths," neither they nor later Akins (1986, 2003) mention that the face of skeleton 14 had been smashed in (Appendix A, plates A.2–A.4). Both understate (scientific caution?) the degree of trauma and what seemed to Nickels and me to be the obvious conclusion that the man represented by skeleton 14 was murdered, as was the case with the other man (skeleton 13) buried beneath the plank floor.

This all raises questions about the circumstances of the attack, which took place elsewhere before the bodies were moved into the tomb toward the rear of Pueblo Bonito. The location of the wounds makes it clear that it came from the front—the attacker was facing the man represented by skeleton 14 and possibly or probably the skeleton 13 individual. But were the individuals sleeping, otherwise unconscious, sitting, or lying face up? The cut marks on the left femur of skeleton 14 indicate that he became aware of the attack at some point before or at the moment his skull was first punctured and before his face was bashed in. There are myriad possibilities but no way to know exactly what happened.

What makes these burials even more intriguing is the context: the wealth of material accompanying the two men, the rich deposits in the fill in Room 33 above the plank floor, the remains of twelve other individuals buried in Room 33 after the two murdered men were placed beneath the plank floor, the person represented by skeleton 14 laid on a prepared surface of yellow sand and wood ashes. If, as Pepper suggests, the two men represented by skeletons 13 and 14 were priests or others of high rank, then the rich funerary grave goods might be seen as atonement for the killings, if done by Pueblo Bonitans, or as accompanying accoutrements for the afterlife if they were killed by non-Bonitans. It must also be noted, as is clear in figures 16–18, that the two men were *not* buried side by side; the individual represented by skeleton 14 was buried first, and the person who was skeleton 13 was buried about two feet (61 cm) above and at an angle across the legs of skeleton 14. Finally, to the best of my knowledge, individuals 13 and 14 were buried with the richest assemblage of grave goods in the Southwest, with the possible exception of the "Burial of an Early American Magician" described by McGregor (1943).

In her later analysis, Kerriann Marden (2011, 312) states that "only four of the individuals in the northern burial complex [Rooms 32–33 and 56] exhibit any skeletal signs that could be interpreted as perimortem violence," and on pages 196 and 203, she attributes most of the damage to the effects of excavation. Admittedly, Pepper was not the most careful excavator by today's standards, but even he could not have inflicted that much damage on the skeletal materials. No, what happened to the men of H/3671 and H/3672 was deliberate violence—"Murder most foul," as in Shakespeare's *Hamlet*.

What are we to make of the twelve bodies placed in the fill above the plank floor? Were they also high-ranking individuals? The ceremonial nature of much of the material placed in Room 33 suggests this possibility. Were they sacrifices to accompany the two men below the floor? There is evidence for human sacrifice in the Southwest, including in the ethnographic record, though the evidence is generally second-hand: for example, the sacrifice of a boy and girl to the Plumed Water Serpent, the Pueblo equivalent of and derivation from Quetzalcoatl, linking rain and the sun's motion across the sky with the necessity for sacrifice; and the origin of the katsinam with the beheading of a boy. (See, e.g., Adolph F. Bandelier in Lange and Riley 1966, 78–80; Bunzel 1932, 609; Curtis 1926, 22, 109; Cushing 1896, 429; Fewkes 1920, 502; Kidder 1958, 227–29; Parsons 1939, 184, 214, 220, 241, 1017; Reyman 1971, 158–59.) Furthermore, Pueblo scalp societies and ceremonies may be attenuated forms of earlier sacrificial rites, and the Laguna Pueblo custom of wearing a piece of an enemy's skin bears a resemblance to the Aztec practice of wearing a flayed man's skin (Parsons 1939, 1017), especially in conjunction with

FIGURE 16

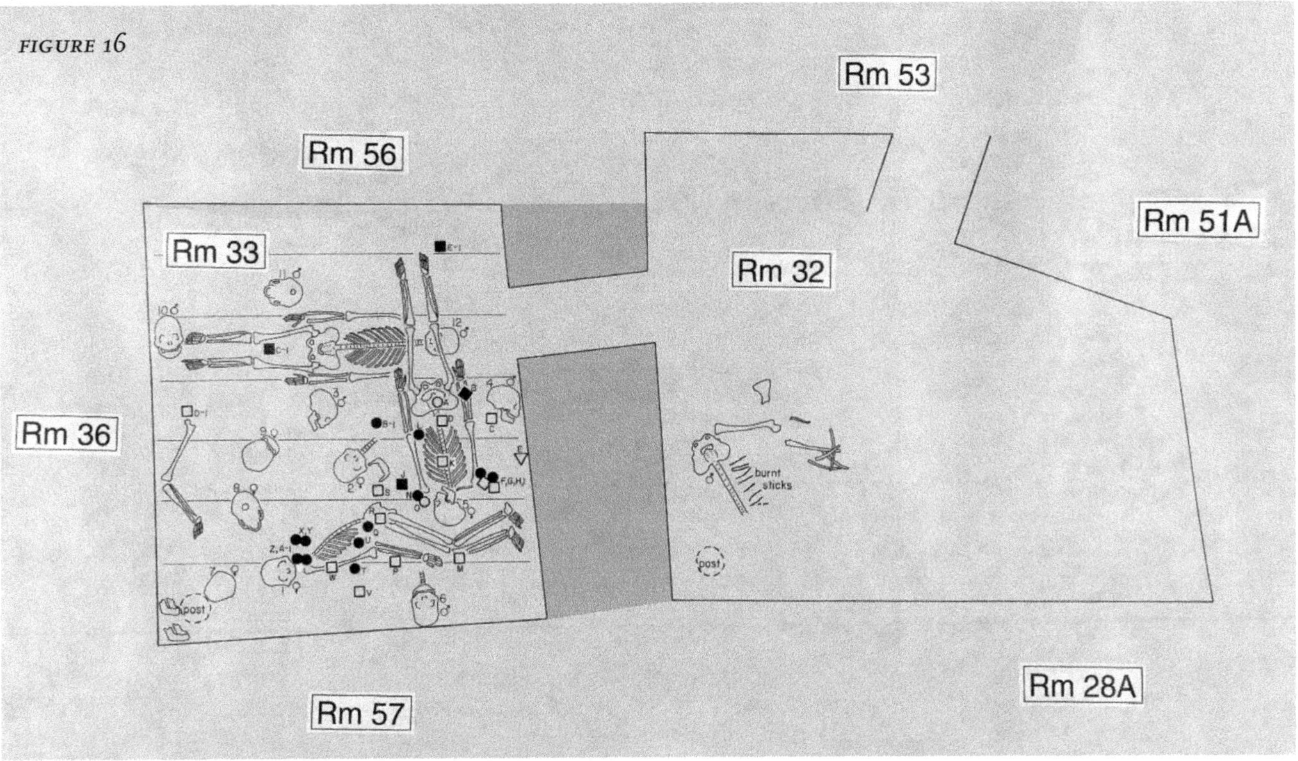

FIGURES 16–18. Three commissioned drawings of Room 33, Pueblo Bonito, by Julianne Snider of the Illinois State Museum. *16*: The complexity of the burials and accompanying artifacts above the plank floor (top) and below the plank floor (bottom). *17*: The complexity of the burials above the plank floor (top) and the positions of the two burials below the plank floor (bottom). *18*: The complexity of the burials below the plank floor.

FIGURE 17

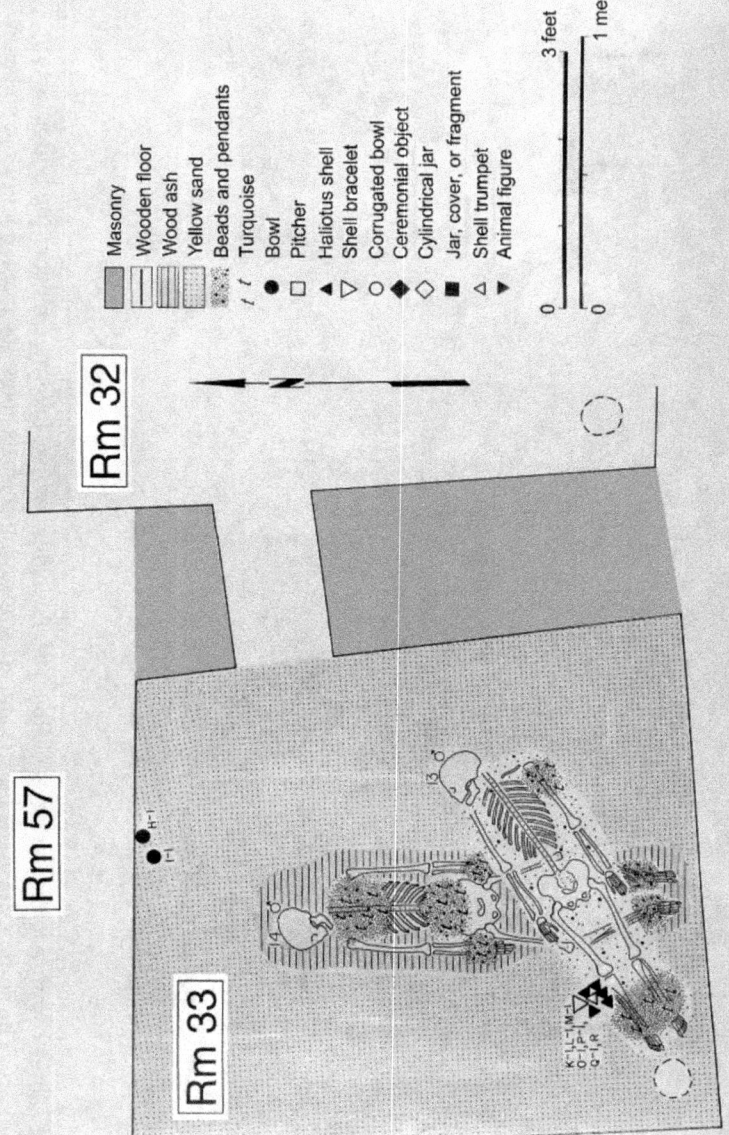

FIGURE 18

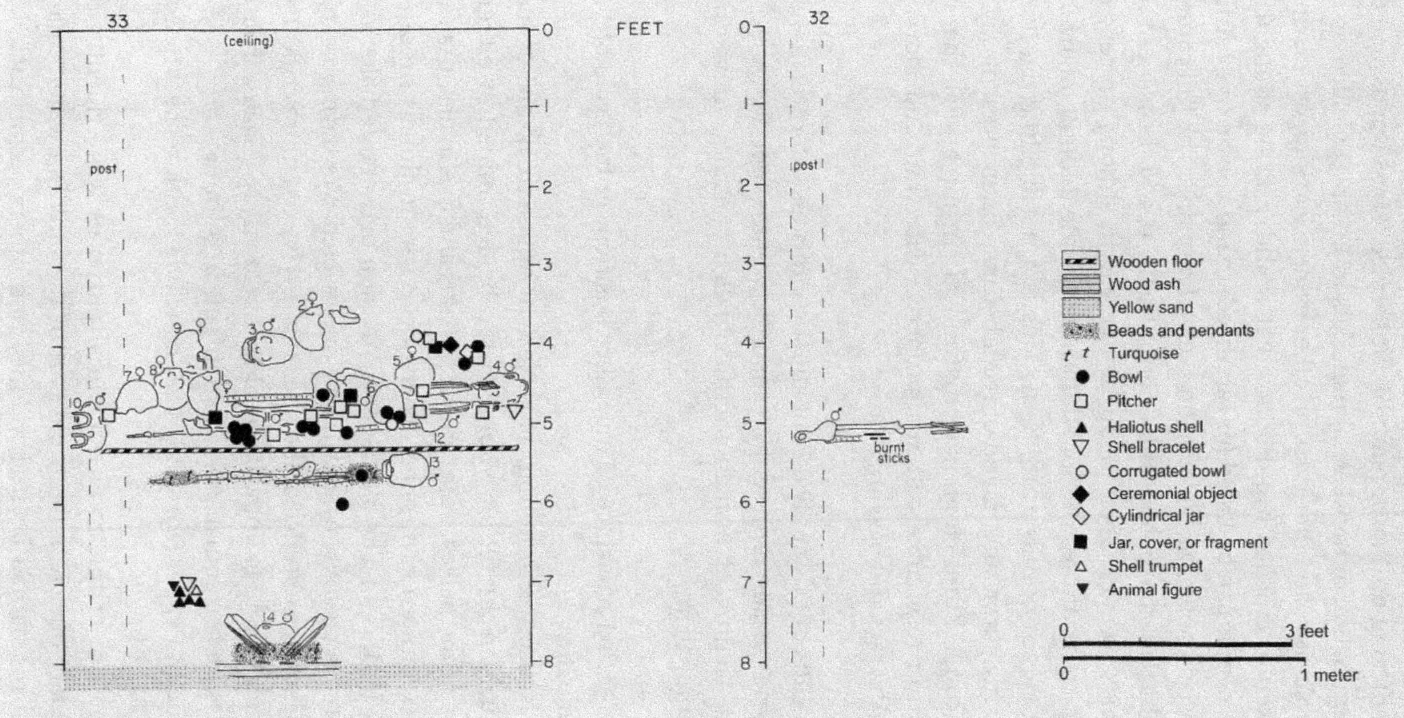
33
(ceiling)
post
FEET
32
post
burnt sticks
Wooden floor
Wood ash
Yellow sand
Beads and pendants
Turquoise
Bowl
Pitcher
Haliotus shell
Shell bracelet
Corrugated bowl
Ceremonial object
Cylindrical jar
Jar, cover, or fragment
Shell trumpet
Animal figure
0
3 feet
0
1 meter

rites centering on the worship of Xipe Totec. However, as noted earlier, our examination of the skeletal materials in Room 33 yielded no evidence of decapitation, and there was no other evidence to suggest sacrifice, such as broken or crushed hyoid bones that would indicate strangulation. Of course, people can be killed (or sacrificed) using poison or by suffocation, but these do not leave evidence on skeletal remains. The full context of the twelve burials above the plank floor in Room 33 and the issues their presence raises remain open for further research, although recent research using DNA indicates the individuals constitute a single matriline (Kennett, et al. 2017; Mills 2018, 8–9). This is a notable finding, though not necessarily surprising in and of itself because many present-day Pueblos (e.g., Acoma, Zuni, Hopi) have matrilineal kinship and all that it entails in terms of residential patterns, property ownership, and more. Marden (2011, Abstract and passim), states:

> Results of this study do not support previous interpretations that these burials represent sociopolitical elites, nor that they were the victims of human sacrifice, fallen warriors, or victims of cannibalism.

Marden (2015) has since changed her position on the issue of the sociopolitical elites.

It is also worth noting, as is clear in Appendix B, that of the eleven individuals in the fill for whom sex can be determined by either cranial features or the pelves, there are six females and five males. (As noted earlier, one cranium is missing, having been sent to Robert Broom in 1914 by Aleš Hrdlička.) The almost even division between females and males struck us as curious, unusual, and unexpected. We have no explanation for this, and the absence of the one cranium is even more critical; it would have been helpful to know its sex. Marden (2011, 193) states that there are six males and six females plus two infants in Room 33.

Finally, Pepper (1909, 247–48) concluded with respect to Room 33:

> The use of this room for burial purposes was evidently a secondary one. It is in an old part of the building, where many of the rooms had been abandoned and others reconstructed. The

surrounding rooms had been taken for burial purposes and for storage of ceremonial material.[11] Although skeletons were found in other parts of the pueblo, none presented conditions similar to those existing in the case under consideration.

As no burial-mounds were in evidence near Pueblo Bonito,[12] and as there were comparatively few rock burials in the vicinity, intramural inhumation was to be expected. But when it is considered that valuable jewelry and ceremonial paraphernalia were buried with practically all of the bodies in this series of rooms, it would seem that in life the deceased must have belonged to the priesthood, and have been buried within the walls of the pueblo both as a mark of respect[13] and as a means of protecting their graves from possible spoliation at the hands of semi-nomadic tribes. The Navaho and the Ute prize ornaments of turquoise above all other possessions; and their greed for this material, both for personal ornament and for use as a medium of exchange, would cause them to go to almost any extreme to obtain it. From the explorations of burial-mounds near pueblos of the Chaco group, it is known that practically no turquoise was buried with the bodies, the non-perishable material being confined almost exclusively to fictile productions. This fact suggests that the pueblos of this region, probably without exception, contain the remains of those who were either members of the priesthood, caciques, or who held other positions of importance in the community.

This is known to be true of Pueblo Bonito and of Peñasca Blanca [sic]; for in both of these pueblos masses of turquoise ornaments have been found associated with bodies buried in rooms, and further research in these and other ruins should result in similar discoveries.

As one reads the analyses by Akins (1966, 2003) and Marden (2011), and Nickels' Appendix B to this volume, while there is general agreement about the number of individuals buried in Rooms 32–33 (fourteen adults, to which Marden, p. 193, adds two infants), it is obvious that there are discrepancies in the specific measurements taken and the result of those measurements, pathologies and other nonmetric traits, and the conditions of burial. These are the results of the time that elapsed between when Akins, Nickels, and I did our studies at the AMNH (1979–1980) and when Marden did her research (ca. 2007–2009). I noted above some differences between the condition of the skeletal materials. There was a comingling of materials during this roughly thirty-year period, the loss or misplacement of some bones, and certainly different ways of looking at and analyzing the remains and interpreting the results. Despite all this, it strikes me that there is more general agreement than disagreement among the four of us, albeit that Marden focused on certain skeletal features and the possible causes of some of their current condition that neither Akins nor we considered. The science has evolved and changed significantly over thirty years, e.g., DNA and other chemical analyses. The dating of the burials in Rooms 32–33 is just one example with which I close the main discussion on these two rooms.

Akins (2003) suggests a deposition period in Rooms 32–33 of about 175 years based on the ceramic styles of pottery found with the burials. As noted earlier, Plog and Heitman (2010) suggest on the basis of radiocarbon dates, notably from burials 13 and 14, that these rooms were among the earliest in use at the site, ca. AD 800, and that "The use of Room 33 as a mortuary chamber dates to the earliest phase of occupation of Pueblo Bonito and continued into the late 11th and possibly early 12th centuries, potentially a span of 300–400 y" (19623). Their AMS base dates are AD 781 for Burial 13 and AD 873 for Burial 14, almost a one-hundred-year difference. Note that Burial 14 is *below* Burial 13 and in the natural order of things should be earlier, not later. For comparison, Brenner et al. (2007, 315–17) have dates of ca. AD 800–1100 for Pueblo Bonito's occupation, and Coltrain et al. (2007) date the rooms to the Pueblo I in the early building period of Pueblo Bonito.

Plog and Heitman (2010), on the basis of various sources, state that "the burials and rich assemblages are widely regarded as dating between AD 1020 and 1100." I agree with this dating. Furthermore, the only other comparable "rich assemblage" comes from the burial of an "Early American Magician" found at Ridge Ruin (McGregor 1943). This is an Eldon Phase site that dates to AD 1070–1275, with the burial likely dating to AD 1150–1250. Although not an eastern Ancestral Pueblo site, its contents are especially comparable for some of the artifact assemblages from Rooms 32–33, especially inlaid objects and what might be called "invested" wood objects. (The Ridge Ruin materials were reburied in 2012 in compliance with Native American Graves Protection and Repatriation Act guidelines, so no further study of the original materials is possible.)

How, then, do we reconcile the early AMS dates for burials 13 and 14 with some of the unquestionably (to my mind) much later objects found with the burials in Rooms 32–33, such as invested flageolets (flutes) and other wood objects, e.g., the "Design Board" (H/4500; Pepper 1920, 156, 158–59) and the hematite bird with turquoise inlay (H/10416; Pepper 1920, 134–35, figure 50)? *If* one accepts the argument that Rooms 32–33 were accessible in some way after the initial construction and for several hundred years thereafter, then the problem disappears. Akins's 175-year span based on pottery styles would represent later offerings to the early ancestors, as would the elaborate decorated items dating to the eleventh century and later. The same could also be true for the huge quantity of turquoise beads buried with those interred, especially individuals 13 and 14. The canes or ceremonial sticks, arrows, etc. may well represent the earliest grave goods or offerings; radiocarbon dating could and probably would resolve this question.

Furthermore, for the sake of completeness, it should be noted that Pepper found human remains or parts of skeletons in Rooms 53, 61, 79, and 80 at Pueblo Bonito. Rooms 53 and 56 had been excavated by Warren K. Moorehead in April 1897 (Moorehead 1906). He did not do a thorough excavation of the rooms, nor was it his intention to do so: "It was not the purpose of Mr. Peabody's expedition to attempt a thorough exploration, but simply to make a typical collection in three weeks, and as a total of about two thousand specimens of various kinds were secured in that time, the object of the visitation was accomplished" (33).

This was the worst kind of "hit-and-run" event posing as archaeology. Additional proof that Moorehead did little more than poke around in Room 53 is evidenced by the fact that, when Pepper excavated the room, he recovered an almost complete postcranial human skeleton, a separate lower mandible, a child's skull, over four thousand flat turquoise beads, thirty shell beads or pendants, various pottery vessels including a portion of a cylinder jar, and a variety of other objects (Pepper 1920, 210–13). Pepper's (1897) unpublished field notes for this room provide architectural construction details but no additional information about the contents. At the AMNH, we found more bones than Pepper reported. We did not do a full count or analysis of them, but Akins (1986, 118) lists "mandibles of two males and a female, the child's skull . . . and two mixed groups of bones that represent a newborn infant, at least one and possibly two adolescents, a male, a female, and another adult."

For Room 61, Pepper (1920, 223) describes the contents as follows:

> Most of the specimens found in this room were in the débris covering the floor; fragments of a human skull, scattered about in the southeast corner; pieces of a jaw with teeth and fragments of a cranium, blackened and charred to such an extent that it seems hardly possible that it could have been accidental. There was no evidence of there having been a fire in this room. The only piece of charred wood found was a section of a post 2 feet long and 2 inches in diameter. This had evidently fallen from one of the upper rooms. The pieces of the skull lay as if they had been scattered by hand. Had they fallen with the debris from the ceiling above, they would not have been lying in the positions they occupied in the accumulation of floor material. There were a few fragments of human bones beside the skull, but these showed no evidence of having been burnt.

Pepper's (1897) unpublished field notes contain a few details that differ from the published description: the post is 3 inches in diameter rather than 2 inches and "evidently had been thrown in" rather than having fallen in. What evidence Pepper had for these two points and why he changed them in the published version are unknown. He also notes that the skull fragments were

> scattered over an area fully four feet in diameter . . . as though they had been scattered by hand [because] had they fallen from the ceiling above they would not have covered so much space and rodents would hardly have carried them around to such an extent.

These differences are again evidence, albeit minor in this case, that Pepper did not publish all his data, and they also provide insight into his methodology and thinking.

Room 79 yielded the burial of a child beneath the floor (Pepper 1920, 264). Although the practice of subfloor interment was relatively common in the Bc (Hosta Butte Phase) sites at Chaco Canyon, it was not at Pueblo Bonito or the other great houses. More important is the architecture of the room itself, which Pepper (1920, 264) described as follows:

> Room 79 is the angular room forming the northwest corner of Estufa [kiva] 75. The estufa is built in a square enclosure, the circular wall touching the wall of the enclosure at four points. The remaining space forms the angular rooms in the corners of the square. The estufa wall formed a convex side to these rooms. The other two sides are straight. As a rule, very little was found in rooms of this nature.

Pepper's unpublished notes for Room 79 add little except a few more details about the construction of the room. However, his description and the contents of Room 79 are evidence that Windes's (personal communication, March 15, 2010) reasoning for excluding firepits (hearths) involves an incorrect assumption about these triangular rooms: "I may have discarded those FP's in rooms that were not really rooms (like odd triangle corners or such that got 'room' designations but were not truly rooms)." Two possibilities must be noted: first, they could have been in rooms that were rebuilt, and second, they may have served as hearths for the adjoining room(s). Regardless, they are *still* hearths and must be counted as such in the final tabulation.

Room 80 contained human bones scattered through the fill, which "had evidently fallen from one of the upper rooms" (Pepper 1920, 267). These bones showed evidence of having been burned and they were broken, as is the case with other human bones found in the pueblos of this group; from the fact that they had been in one of the upper rooms, it may be that they were used for some ceremonial purpose, as it was not the custom to bury even portions of bodies in the upper rooms. At least, no other evidences of such a practice were found.

In his conclusions, Pepper (1920, 378) suggested that the evidence of burned bones in Rooms 61 and 80—fifteen skeletal elements according to Marden (2011, 2295)—and the finding of large numbers of charred and cracked bones at Peñasco Blanco by a Navajo worker named Waylo (Pepper 1899a) raise the possibility of cannibalism at Chaco Canyon. Room 80 is notable because it contained the famous "Painted Stone Mortar"—"the most elaborately decorated object of this nature that was found in the pueblo" (Pepper 1920, 264–67, figures 109 and 110; see plate 3) and one of many objects decorated in a decidedly Mesoamerican technique, in my opinion (Reyman 1990).

Pepper's unpublished 1897 field notes contain two important data not found in the published report. First, Pepper determined that Room 80 had upper and lower floor levels; and "about a dozen metates were left on the [lower] floor level of this room placed there for future use." Second, this room was filled with numerous stone tools (e.g., fifty-three hammerstones and thirty-one manos), pottery and pottery fragments, bone and antler tools, a stone jar cover, animal bones, and more, all of which makes the presence of the burned human bone anomalous. Unfortunately, the additional details provided in the unpublished field notes do not help to explain the contents or function of this room, which Pepper seems to think was some kind of workshop. Pepper (1899a) also found a small area, behind and west of Pueblo Bonito and just east of the stairway up the mesa, with a thin (¼") layer of charcoal, a thicker one of ashes, and then more charcoal mixed with pottery fragments and other debris. He notes the remains of a fireplace and speculates that the area may have served as a camp site. However, that this directly follows the discussion of charred human bones at Pueblo Bonito and Peñasco Blanco makes one wonder whether Pepper was implicitly suggesting that the area/feature served as a crematory or for cooking human parts for cannibalism.

Finally, Neil M. excavated a complex of four burial rooms (320, 326, 329, and 330) in the western portion of Pueblo Bonito, occupied by what Judd termed the "Old Bonitans" (Judd 1954, 325–42, plates 91–99). Although he does not say so explicitly, reading his description makes it clear that these rooms did not have access to the outside, or to other

PLATE 3. The pseudo-cloisonné "Painted Stone Mortar" from Room 80, Pueblo Bonito. *Photo*: Jonathan E. Reyman.

rooms, although there were limited possibilities to get from one room to another. The presence of a flagstone floor in Room 320, an unusual feature, led Judd to infer that the room had been designed for storage (325).

Akins (1984, 119) writes (and I agree with her regarding her frustration):

> Working with Judd's (1954) report on the Pueblo Bonito burials is a frustrating experience . . . Much of the information is missed if only Judd's section on the burials (1954, 325–41) is considered. Some objects and individual burials are well described, but it is only when the provenience of the illustrated objects and the section on dress and adornment are reviewed that it becomes clear that much is left out of the description. It was necessary to use the [unpublished] U.S. National Museum catalogue to compile a list of the contents of the rooms, and even then much of the information is not quantified.[14]

With regard to the flagstone floor, she states: "The room may have been set aside for burials, as a four-strand turquoise necklace was found coiled with two pairs of pendants between two stones and covered with plaster" (119). From this, Akins seems to suggest that the necklace and pendants were a sealed offering, perhaps meant to sanctify the room for the dead who were to be placed within it some time later. I suggest another possibility: that these objects were sealed in the floor, perhaps as offerings, in the same way that necklaces, pendants, and beads were sealed into wall niches of the Great Sanctuary at Chetro Ketl (Hewett 1936a, 87–94), and that the necklace and pendants were earlier and unrelated to the burials placed in the room.

The presence of fireplaces and ventilators in Rooms 329 and 330 led Judd to conclude that the two rooms had been originally intended as the loci of "secret societies" and "esoteric rites" (1954, 331–33). Given that human remains were buried in these rooms above the level of the fireplaces and ventilator openings, one must assume that the societies and their rites found other homes or ceased to exist. Judd (1964, 58) further states:

The quantity and diversity of ceremonial paraphernalia stored in some of those small rooms suggest an importance in the community quite out of proportion to their size. And four of them [320, 326, 329, 330] had come eventually to be used for burials—priesthood burials if one may judge from the wealth of accompanying contents.

Judd (1954, 334) originally states that sixty-eight burials came from Rooms 320, 326, 329, and 330, and that just over 67 percent were disturbed. He also notes (325) that the National Geographic Society's excavations at Pueblo Bonito yielded a total of seventy-three skeletons. However, in his second report (Judd 1964, 64) he indicates that seventy-three skeletons came from the four burial rooms. Either Judd confused the situation or perhaps he did a recount between his writing of the first and second reports.

Regardless, neither number is correct. Admittedly, skeletal analysis advanced greatly between the years Judd worked and the 1980s: Akins (1986, 119) reports that Palkovich (1984) identified twenty-one skeletons from Room 320 in comparison to ten or eleven reported by Judd (1954, 325–26), and Palkovich (1984, 104), in a reanalysis of the materials, lists 112 individuals excavated by Judd and retained in the Smithsonian's collections. One implication is that Judd did not retain all skeletal remains excavated, so the number of individuals may have been higher. This supports my argument that unpublished materials and existing collections are important sources of primary data. Palkovich also states:

> Given that these rooms [320, 326, 329, 330] are roughly contemporaneous and are immediately adjacent to each other in the Pueblo Bonito room complex, it can be argued that this area represents a formal "cemetery" or at least is the closest thing to a spatially distinct, temporally discrete interment area noted to date in Chaco Canyon (Palkovich 1984, 104).

I do not dispute Palkovich's statement, but as shown below, there were formal cemeteries in the form of burial mounds in Chaco Canyon as opposed to house and trash mounds. Pepper and Wetherill discovered many and excavated several.

There is no question that many internments excavated by Judd had been disturbed; he provides ample descriptive and photographic evidence to support this (Judd 1954, 325–42, plates 91, 92, 96, 97, 99). In some cases, e.g., Room 330, the cause of the disturbance is given as ancient vandalism or grave robbing and the "[l]ack of turquoise ornaments and, indeed, the paucity of ornaments of any kind, suggest a motivating reason for the vandalism" (335). In Room 326, he rules out vandalism because nearby skeletons were undisturbed and explains the disturbance thus: "That the head and limbs of No. 11 had been pulled from the trunk may, as a guess, be attributed to the jittery haste with which preparations were made for a later burial" (330). He further states:

> Sepulture is a fearful task the Pueblo assumes unwillingly and concludes as speedily as possible. It is dread of what might happen rather than callousness that motivates grave diggers at modern Zuñi, for example, where each new grave in the crowded churchyard disturbs half a dozen deceased relatives and one-time neighbors. Get the job done and get away! So uprooted bones are anxiously scraped in on top of the latest corpse and covered with a bare foot or two of earth (330).

My own experience at Zuni and Acoma is somewhat similar in that previous burials may be moved aside when a newly deceased person is to be interred in the Campo Santo at the old mission church, which apparently does sometimes result in a comingling of individuals and materials. But I'm unaware of the attendant *fear* reported by Judd, or perhaps none of my Pueblo friends and colleagues at the two Pueblo villages saw fit to mention it.

Akins, however, does not fully accept Judd's argument. She notes (1986, 125):

> Pepper's disturbed burials had a large number of ornaments, much more than Judd's undisturbed burials. Judd's report gives the impression that the undisturbed burials were usually laid out on a surface and then covered with soil or debris, rather than being actual interments. Disturbance that can be attributed to

intrusion of one grave into another appears to have been minimal and was suggested by Judd only once as a possible cause.

Without detailed notes and drawings, it is difficult to account for all that went on. However, Pepper's rooms in particular [e.g., Room 80] and some of Judd's may have held secondary burials. The discrepancy between Hrdlička's counts (based only on skulls) and Palkovich's (based on all elements) suggests that, while some burials were in place, others may have been moved in various stages of decomposition (cf. Plog and Heitman 2019; Marden 2011). Grave robbers may have done more damage to the skeletons themselves, yet there is little breakage. Secondary burial combined with a variety of phenomena such as rodent and carnivore activity, trash deposition, and the effects of rain is at least as plausible as previous explanations. I would add that a close reading of Judd's (1954, 325–37) description of the contents in the four burial rooms and careful viewing of the accompanying photographs (plates 91–99) clearly indicate that grave goods were present with a number of the disturbed burials. Furthermore, undisturbed burials were found in the same room with disturbed ones, as in the case of Rooms 320 and 326. If grave robbing were the cause of the disturbance, why would the vandals not have thoroughly gone through the entire contents of the rooms? Why do half the job? I suggest that interments of later burials and secondary burials, combined with the factors noted by Akins (above), constitute a reasonable explanation.

In an attempt to resolve Akins's frustration and confusion, and mine, I spent several days in the Smithsonian attics and other places in the museum reading Judd's unpublished notes and other materials. There is a great deal of information there, but none of it that I read (and there may be materials I missed or *didn't* read) helped to clarify the frustrating, confused situation. Indeed, the vast majority that I did read were, at best, tangential to my research, and I decided there was no point in publishing these data, in contrast to the Pepper–Wetherill materials. Once again, I wished for a time machine to take me back so that I could talk with Pepper, Wetherill, Hewitt, Judd, and others, or, better yet, to go to Chaco Canyon and especially to Pueblo Bonito to observe. A question to myself: was anything at Chaco Canyon even close to the painting on the cover of this book?

CHAPTER FOUR

Burial Mounds and Cemeteries

TO BEGIN THE DISCUSSION of burial mounds and cemeteries, it must be reiterated that, although George Pepper and Richard Wetherill were puzzled about the location of the burials specifically from Pueblo Bonito, they found no general paucity of burials in general. Pepper discusses this in his Conclusion section to *Pueblo Bonito*:

> The use of certain rooms for burial purposes seems to have been secondary . . . An extensive cemetery has been found west of and near Pueblo Pintado . . . Similar conditions should obtain in the case of Bonito and the other large pueblos of the Chaco Cañon (Pepper 1920, 376).

In fact, Pepper and Wetherill did find numerous burials in mounds across the arroyo from Pueblo Bonito and in other parts of the canyon and its environs in addition to the aforementioned cemetery near Pueblo Pintado. One of the largest, Mound 5, is discussed below.

I also noted earlier Marietta Wetherill's description of a burial mound (Appendix A, figure A.2) to Gordon Vivian, indicating that it was but one of a number that covered several acres. It is worth rereading her account in chapter 3 for the purpose of this discussion.

In one respect, Marietta Wetherill's statement is difficult to take at face value: it is unlikely that any single burial mound would have been acres in extent. This would be as large as or larger than Chetro Ketl, the largest Chaco Canyon pueblo in terms of surface area at more than 250,000 square feet, or about 5.7 acres (Vivian and Hilpert 2002, 75). Given all the archaeology conducted at Chaco Canyon over more than a century, one would surely expect that a burial mound acres in extent would have been found. Perhaps what she meant is that the sum total of the bones, ashes, and pottery dispersed throughout the canyon covered several acres. Given the size of Mound 5 and other burial mounds recorded by Pepper and Wetherill, this seems a more reasonable possibility.[1]

In some ways, the following account by Marietta Wetherill, also recorded by Gordon Vivian (1948), is even more intriguing:

> To add to the stories of things found at Bonito—On the west side was a large square room. In one corner was an extended burial of a man. Strands of turquoise beads were wrapped around his forehead. Long strings of turquoise were looped around his shoulders and hung down to his waist. There was almost a bushel of turquoise on this fellow. Around the wall were 13 skeletons of women. None with any ornaments [cf. Akins and Schelberg 1984, 91].

After quoting this description, Vivian commented:

> You'll remember that Pepper's [1920] report says something about "The burial rooms in Pueblo Bonito are covered in my separate report in some other publication" [Pepper 1909]. I asked Mrs. Wetherill about these burial rooms. She says there weren't any. She definitely does not like Pepper [this is twenty-seven years after Pepper's death]. She said he was "a very queer young man" [and] the less she hears about him the better.

One is tempted to think that Mrs. Wetherill was confused, that the above account is actually about the finds in Rooms 32–33: The vast amount of turquoise and the accompanying burials remind one of the contents of the two burial rooms. However, there are sufficient differences in the details to suggest that this was a separate find: The room was on the west side of Pueblo Bonito, not the north side; there were no strands of turquoise around the forehead and shoulders; and the accompanying burials in Rooms 32–33 were about equally divided between men and women.

Nevertheless, Pepper makes no mention of this find in either his publications or his unpublished notes and field diaries. If Wetherill excavated the room independently of the Hyde Exploring Expedition work, he makes no mention of it in *his* unpublished notes. So where are the skeletal remains and the bushel of turquoise? I have no answers, but we do know that at one point Wetherill rode to Farmington to retrieve turquoise (and other materials?) stolen by a Navajo worker from a Chaco site, possibly Pueblo Bonito or Peñasco Blanco.

Richard Wetherill had running disagreements with Navajo workers and canyon residents, which may well have been a factor in his 1910 murder by Chis-chillin-Begay (see McNitt 1966). As for Marietta Wetherill's attitude toward Pepper, her husband also seems to have felt dislike or resentment toward him almost from the outset of the Hyde Exploring Expedition. Wetherill was fifteen years older than Pepper and an experienced, internationally known archaeological explorer. Pepper was a neophyte in the Southwest, but also Wetherill's supervisor. This apparently did not sit well with Wetherill, though he did work with Pepper and followed his instructions. One indication that the two men did not like each other, and perhaps a contributing factor to Mrs. Wetherill's attitude toward Pepper in her 1948 meeting with Vivian is that when Richard was ambushed and murdered in 1910, Pepper never sent a letter, note, or telegram of condolence to Marietta.

Most of the information on burial mounds and cemeteries discovered by the Hyde Exploring Expedition remains unpublished. One of the best general accounts, though not without problems, is in Pepper's 1899 lecture notes. As before, there are words in brackets [ ] indicating that Pepper edited his notes or changed what he said during the course of the lecture, perhaps depending upon his audience. Words in parentheses ( ) are my editing:

> We will now leave Pueblo Bonito for a few minutes and cross the plain to the large burial mound, that I pointed out on the south side of the cañon: we will here obtain an idea of the manner of inhumation in the mounds that may be contrasted later with the room burials of Bonito, which are the only ones found in connection with that ruin. This burial mound is simply the soil that has

PLATE 4

PLATES 4 and 5. 1974 photographs of Richard (1910) and Marietta (1948) Wetherill's burial site in a cemetery east of Pueblo Bonito. This burial area may lie atop an ancient Chacoan burial mound. Note the misspelling of Richard's last name. *Photos*: Jonathan E. Reyman.

---

washed down from the mesa and formed a deposit, from two to three feet in depth, on the rocky slope below[2]: it was here that the skeletons were found, the gentleman (presumably either Richard Wetherill or a Navajo field worker) standing near the center of the mounds. The method [*plan*] of procedure, when a mound of this kind is to be explored, is to make a regular plan with divisions in the form of squares: the work is then begun [*commenced*] and when a specimen is reached, a triangulation is made from two of the corners of the section in which it is found and is then uncovered and photographed in situ. A great many skeletons were found in this place, but I will simply show you a few of them in order that you may get a general conception of what field work involves, under a tropical sun that causes the thermometer to register 130° in the shade. When a skeleton was found the loose dirt was removed from above it, by the men, and then I gave it my personal attention, the implements being a small trowel, a steel stylus, and a series of brushes: each bone was cleared and brought out in strong relief, without being moved, and then the photograph was taken: the uncovering process would, at times, necessitate the most careful application for hours, and that too in the glare of the suns (sic) rays which were reflected from the sand as from a mirror. This skeleton is represented by only a few bones, but the vessels are in place and are, bar[r]ing the deposit of soda ash that covers the surface, evidently as perfect as when they were buried.

A general custom seemed to prevail in this region, concerning the arrangement of the pottery: when a number of pieces were buried with a body, most of them were grouped about the head or near the shoulders, as shown in this picture, and therefore one can generally tell where the vessels would be from the position of the skeleton.

You may now obtain an insight into the actual methods adopted in the field: the dirt is thrown back as we advance and each find is carefully measured and its position indicated on the plan, then the individual skeletons are photographed for their special characteristics after which the groups are taken, which shows us, not only the relation of the pottery to the skeletons, but also the positions of the burials and their environments.

The usual form of burial is brought before us in this picture: in most cases, the bodies were placed in the grave with the knees bent upward, toward the chin: this made a compact mass and relieved the people of the necessity of digging a long grave, which, with their crude tools, would have been quite laborious: the custom, however, may have had a religious meaning. All the graves must have been marked, in some way, as no superimposed bodies were found: in fact, some of the graves had a stone at either the

PLATE 5

head or the feet: the skeletons, in some graves, almost touched, but in no instance did they overlap. This picture shows the burials in the Northern part of the mound: five bodies being in evidence.

Before leaving this part of the cañon, we will view the scene of the operations from the South mesa. On the extreme right is the mound in which the skeletons were found, and near it the small ruin of the house in which the people probably lived: Just west of this point there is a ridge that is made prominent by the line of greasewood bushes: then on the western slope of the ridge there is a large circular ruin (Casa Rinconada): the black line that crosses the picture laterally is the arroyo, or water course, that serves to conduct the water from the Eastern water shed, to the Escavada at the mouth of the canon: at the right of the picture, and in the mouth of a branch canyon, Pueblo Chettro Kettle may be seen, and at the left, Pueblo Bonito, while above and North of the latter, on the mesa, is Pueblo Alto.

After completing the work in this burial mound, we selected another about a mile west of it at the mouth of the branch canon that enters the Chaco from the South. This view, taken from the North cliff, shows us Pueblo del Arroyo as well as the burial mound (plates 6–7): through this break in the mesa, the San Mateo mountains may be seen, on a clear day, also the towering peak of Mt. Tailor (*sic*).

In the second burial mound, stone graves, or cysts, were found: the picture on the screen giving a fair idea of their appearance. Had all the bodies been laid away in these boxes of imperishable material, our work would have been comparatively easy, but when one searches for hours for a skeleton, that the presence of pottery would cause one to expect, and then find[s] only a few teeth, as was the case with the burial here shown, it resolves itself into a problem that keeps one thinking.

An interesting skeleton was found near the surface of this mound: in fact, the earth had washed away to such an extent that the femora protruded from the soil (cf. figure 7 and the description by Marietta Wetherill of another burial mound cited above—Appendix A, figure A.2), and, as may be seen, the ends had been crushed and broken by the sheep and horses that used the place as a grazing ground.

To clear a skeleton for photographing is not only a very delicate and tedious task, but one that is very trying: it is warm work when a body is before you, but when only scattered bones are found, as in this case, the complications that arise seem to materially increase the penetrating force of the suns (*sic*) rays.

The scattering of the bones is due to the erratic wanderings and eccentricities of the mountain of pack rats: here is a skeleton that evidently lay in the path of one of these little animals, for three of the vertebrae are missing: the nest of the rodent was found a few feet beyond and its presence served to verify our theories concerning the stray parts of the human anatomy that were found in various places which were widely removed from the burials.

A peculiar freak of the rats was the displacement of an entire skeleton, at least as much of it as had not decayed, and leaving only a portion of the skull and the crossbone, which may be seen in the right hand corner of the picture: had this man been a pirate, the arrangement could not have been more appropriate.

We now have before us the Bone Diggers and the Grave Robbers, in other words, the principals of two of the Museum expeditions of 1896, Dr. Wortman and party.

Pepper's *Pueblo Bonito* concludes with a fairly lengthy description (pages 339–51) of thirty skeletons excavated by the Hyde Exploring Expedition from two mounds on the south side of the canyon, the first of which "was located on the southern side of Chaco Cañon and Southwest of Pueblo Chettro Kettle" (339). It yielded eleven skeletons and a portion of a crushed cranium. This was Mound 1 in Pepper's unpublished 1896 field notes, on which he began work on June 1, 1896 (Pepper 1896a, 1896b, 42). Akins (1986, 9, 17) identifies Mound 1 as Bc-59, where, in 1950, Ruins Stabilization Unit work uncovered the remains of forty-one individuals. Akins does not explain her identification of Mound 1 as Bc-59, and I am not certain she is correct. Indeed, there is unpublished evidence to the contrary that Mound 1, though approximately 100 feet south of the mound of the Bc-59 house block in 1896, is *not* Bc-59.

First, the Hyde Exploring Expedition photograph (HEE 011, now at the American Museum of Natural History), depicts Wetherill's brother-in-law Orion Buck standing atop a low mound. Pepper's notes state that the mound is on the south side of Chaco Canyon (across the Chaco Wash) and about midway between Pueblo Bonito and Chetro Ketl. Second, Pepper describes the mound as having soil only a few feet deep and comprised mostly of soil that washed off the mesa. This statement indicates that the mound is low, too low to be either the mound of Bc-59 or its refuse mound. Pepper notes that Orion Buck is standing in the center of that part of the mound excavated by Richard Wetherill and Sidney Palmer (Marietta Wetherill's father) a few months before Pepper arrived at Chaco

Canyon in May of 1896. According to Pepper (1896a, 1896b) and judging by other Hyde Exploring Expedition photographs, the location of Mound 1 was about 100 feet or so south of the mound that was Bc-59. It seems reasonable to conclude that Mound 1 was not Bc-59.

Pepper (1920, 341) wrote:

> Our next place of operation was a burial mound near the mouth of the cañon that runs south from Chaco. It is on the right hand side facing south and is in reality in the Chaco limits.

This was a large mound: Pepper laid out an east–west line for forty feet and divided it into five parts to produce five eight-foot sections. Four skeletons were recovered, but Pepper writes that he found the work unproductive (lacking in grave goods), so a new section of the mound was gridded—forty feet long but running north–south and perpendicular to the west end of the first trench (341–47). A total of nineteen skeletons were excavated from this second trench (341–51) before the work ceased. Many or most of the skeletons were in poor condition, such that they crumbled to the touch (350), and there was a paucity of grave goods. There is some question about the lack of material in the mound's second trench; Pepper notes (341) that Wetherill had earlier dug in this mound, and it is certainly within the realm of possibility that Wetherill removed the better grave goods for sale. It must be remembered that Richard Wetherill and his family lived and worked in the canyon (figures 6–7), whereas Pepper came out each year in late spring from New York City and stayed through the fall for the excavation season.

The two trenches in the mound produced a total of thirty or thirty-one individuals that Akins (1986, 164) includes in her table B.1. She lists the excavations as *two* different mounds but not as burial mounds; rather, she assigns them as Bc-117 and Bc-118, or possibly the latter as 29SJ383, as noted in endnote 3 of chapter 3. Akins gives no explanation for this assignment other than her belief, noted above, that she thinks Pepper and Wetherill misidentified house sites as burial mounds. McKenna and Truell (1986, 499) identify Bc-118 as 29SJ383 and describe its location as "at west side right at mouth of South Gap; only the lower mound is included here—the upper mound is now 29SJ393; 12± rooms, 1–2 kivas; PI through PIII."

There are two points worth making here. Admittedly, the location cited by McKenna and Truell is similar to Pepper's "next place of operation" as described on page 341 of *Pueblo Bonito*. Nevertheless, there are several sites in this general area, as is clear in McKenna and Truell's comment about the upper mound. Therefore, one cannot be certain that the mound described by Pepper is the same site as Bc-118 or 29SJ383. The same is true of Akins's designation of the first mound as Bc-117.

The second point is that Bc-117 and Bc-118 or 29SJ383 have masonry architecture; however, Pepper does not mention any kind of masonry architecture either in his published account (1920, 339–51) or his lecture notes that refer to the mounds. It might be argued that Pepper excavated and recovered the skeletal material and grave goods from the trash mounds for these sites, but he never refers to the mounds as trash mounds or middens, and as discussed above, both he and Wetherill knew the difference and became more cognizant of it as the work progressed over several years. By the time Pepper wrote out his lecture notes in 1899, he certainly had a detailed knowledge of the difference, yet he makes it clear that he excavated *burial* mounds.

In April of 1897, Warren K. Moorehead also excavated what he called a small cemetery at Chaco Canyon but gives no indication of its directional location with reference Pueblo Bonito other than about a mile away:

> After the expedition had collected such things as could be found on the surface, a small cemetery about a mile from the principal ruin [Pueblo Bonito] was explored. At a depth of one half to one meter were found a number of skeletons and forty or fifty jars, bowls, etc. Some of these [objects] are illustrated in Figures 10, 11, 12, 13 and 15 (Moorehead 1906, 34).

He does not describe the skeletal materials, but there are three crania from Chaco Canyon at Harvard's Peabody Museum that may be from Moorehead's 1897 excavation (#57024, 57035, and 57049—not shown here). What makes these crania noteworthy is that all three show evidence of blunt-force trauma that almost certainly resulted in the individuals' deaths. These are in addition to the skulls of individuals 13 and 14 found beneath the plank floor in Room 33. Relatively speaking, there seems to have been a *lot* of violence at Chaco Canyon during the height of its occupation.

Akins (1986, 7) cites Moorehead's statement as is, but a couple of pages later, in table 2.1 (9), she lists the "cemetery [as] 1 mile east of Pueblo Bonito." She provides no reason for adding the direction to the cemetery, and I found no indication of its direction relative to Pueblo Bonito in Moorehead's unpublished notes. Perhaps Akins thought Moorehead's cemetery was one of the burial mounds identified by William Strover on his 1906 map (discussed in chapter 2). Given that Stover resurveyed an area that included from just *west* of Pueblo del Arroyo to just *east* of Chetro Ketl, the cemetery excavated by Moorehead, if one mile *east* of Pueblo Bonito, as per Akins, it would *not* have been included in that area. However, given Moorehead's lack of location specificity in the brief citation above, and Strover's 1906 map, this is no more than speculation on my part.

Other unpublished human remains from Chaco Canyon and specifically Pueblo Bonito are in institutions throughout the United States. The Field Museum of Natural History, for example, has seventeen specimens listed in its Skeletal Catalogue (#42519–42535). Nickels and I discovered these while working at the museum in 1988. They had been given to the Field Museum by Nels Nelson in 1943 when he was at the American Museum of Natural History and are in addition to the Pueblo Bonito individuals given to them earlier (1897) by Moorehead. Akins (1986, 9, passim) records most of these.

The actual number of individuals represented by these seventeen catalogue numbers is questionable. The remains are incomplete and usually represented by only one or two bones. For example, #42519 has two right humeri and so must be two individuals. Catalogue #42526 consists of twenty ribs, and #42530 is a sternum. For #42532 there is only a tibia, but it fits so well with the rest of the skeleton catalogued as #42520 that we believe it is part of that individual. In summary, the seventeen Field Museum catalogue numbers include at least seventeen individuals but perhaps twenty or a few more.

FIGURE 19. 1896 Pepper–Wetherill photograph of Casa Rinconada with two small burial mounds to the west of it. The arrows point to Mound 1 (top) and Mound 2 (bottom).

SMALL BURIAL MOUNDS

Wetherill apparently first excavated a small burial mound in 1895 (McNitt 1966, 335), the year before the Hyde Exploring Expedition began work in Chaco Canyon. Pepper's unpublished 1896 field diary indicates that Wetherill and the Palmers (Marietta Wetherill's family) excavated what Pepper (1896b; 1920, 339) designated as Mound 1. Once Pepper arrived in May of 1896, he and Wetherill excavated burial mounds almost from the outset of their work together, alternating between this and putting a trench through the trash mound in front of Pueblo Bonito (Pepper 1896a: 27–48). Two of these small mounds were across the arroyo, just east of Casa Rinconada (figure 19). Yet given the time spent digging these mounds, there is little in Pepper's published papers that discusses the work.[3]

CHAPTER FOUR

Aside from his 1909 paper on Rooms 32–33 at Pueblo Bonito and the material mentioned above in *Pueblo Bonito* (Pepper 1920, 339–51), Pepper published little about the work in burial mounds. The first mention occurs early in Pepper 1920:

> The refuse heap in front of the pueblo, which is to the south, was worked on in an endeavor to discover whether burials had been made in it. There are two refuse heaps in front of the ruin. A large one, which was partly explored and a smaller one to the east of it. After the refuse heaps had been examined, attention was directed to the burial mounds near the base of the mesa on the southern side of the cañon. Two of these mounds were mapped and all of the burials in them photographed and the specimens removed. As this part of the work has no special bearing on the investigation of Pueblo Bonito it will be left for the final chapters of the report [pp. 339–51]. When the excavations in the mounds were finished the actual work in the pueblo was begun (26–27).

However, as noted above, Pepper's unpublished diary (1896a) indicates that other crew members worked on the refuse mounds while Pepper and Wetherill, and occasionally a Navajo worker and Orion Buck, excavated the two burial mounds. Pepper also made brief mentions of burials found in a few rooms in Pueblo Bonito: a pelvis and vertebrae were found in Room 32 (1920, 138) that Marden (2011) stated came from an individual in Room 33; his discussion of the burials in Room 33 (1920, 163–83) is mostly about the accompanying deposits of grave goods. Other examples in Rooms 53 and 80 were discussed earlier.

The excerpt above from Pepper's lecture notes (1899b) refers to the "large circular ruin" just to the west that is known as Casa Rinconada. Across the ridge on the east side are two small burial mounds (see figure 19) that Pepper and Wetherill partly excavated. Unfortunately, neither the notes nor photographs from the excavation of these two mounds seem to have survived, but neither of the two is Mound 1, excavation of which began on June 1, 1896, and which is discussed by Pepper in *Pueblo Bonito* (339).[4] Alternately, perhaps the burials and the accompanying grave goods were so lacking in interest that neither man saw fit to record the information, a situation similar to Pepper's statement for Pueblo Bonito Rooms 116 to 190:

> Nothing of special interest was developed in these excavations aside from the specimens shown in Figures 138 to 154 (1920, 339).

Richard Wetherill's unpublished field notes (1896) include accounts of four burial mounds and their general locations but provide no reason for the gaps between numbers. The locations and descriptions also do not match the numbers in Pepper's unpublished notes, most notably for Pepper's Mound 5, discussed below. Wetherill's Mounds 5 and 8 are no longer extant.

> Burial Mound #3—¾ mile south west of Pueblo Arroya [sic] in side canon of Chaco [Possibly Pepper's Mound 1 (1920, 339)].

> Burial Mound #5—Situated on the south side of Chaco Cañon ¾ mile west of Pueblo Arroya—one of the small house finds the mound nearest the cliff.[5]

> Burial Mound #6—100 yards north of Burial Mound 1 and 50 yards N. East of large Estufa [Casa Rinconada]—the burial place for small house NE of Estufa.[6]

> Burial Mound 8—Almost 100 yards NE of Burial Mound 1, 6 yards SE of House to N West edge of mound.[7]

LARGE BURIAL MOUNDS

Up to this point the discussion has focused on what were probably small burial mounds, although Mound 2 discussed by Pepper (1920, 341) was large enough that he initially laid out five sections of eight-foot-square grids and then subsequently laid out another section forty feet long, probably also with eight-foot-square sections, perpendicular to the first. This would seem to be a large mound, or at least relatively large, though not as large as Mound 5 (figure 7).

One must be cautious in reading Pepper's published reports and unpublished notes, because he occasionally interchanges the terms "burial mounds" and "cemeteries." The same is true for reports by others. For example, Marietta Wetherill's account of burial mounds (Vivian 1948), cited earlier, clearly refers to what, in her perception, were large mounds, some "acres in extent." These would be exceptionally large, indeed, and as noted, are unlikely to have existed—or if they did, would certainly have been found by later fieldworkers. By contrast, the small cemetery excavated by Moorehead (1906, 34) could have been one of the burial mounds noted by William Strover on the 1906 resurvey map discussed above.

Pepper (1920, 376) notes: "An extensive cemetery has been found west of and near Pueblo Pintado." My field crew and I worked at Pueblo Pintado and surveyed the area up to a mile west of it in the summer of 1974 and again in the summer of 1976—in case blowing sand might have uncovered something we missed the first time—but found no trace of a cemetery, nor of burial mounds. We undertook the same sort of search in a wide area around Peñasco Blanco in summer 1974 and in 1976 looking for cemeteries reported in the unpublished literature, as had been done decades earlier (Maher 1947), and with a similar lack of success to that which he reports.

Pepper and Wetherill apparently located several large mounds and excavated at least two or three, one of which was designated Mound 5 in Pepper's unpublished field notes and photographs (see figure 7 and Appendix A, figures A.3–A.8). An indication of the mounds' significant size is found in Wetherill's 1896 unpublished field notes: he states that in one mound they uncovered at least ten burials in a one-meter-by-three-meter trench. Another, much larger mound south of Pueblo del Arroyo (probably Mound 5, which is actually east-southeast of Pueblo del Arroyo) was so large that sixty-four eight-foot-square grids did not cover its entirety. Wetherill (1896) writes that in a single trench in Mound 5, they uncovered forty skeletons. One wonders how many more burials were in this mound, and in the others that Pepper and Wetherill excavated and then abandoned when there were few interesting accompanying grave goods.

In the summer of 1982, I examined 1:3000 aerial photographs of the site at the Southwest Cultural Resource Center at the University of

New Mexico and found what I believe are the remnants of the excavation units still faintly visible for the remaining portion of the mound. Many other important Chacoan architectural and cultural features noted by the Hyde Exploring Expedition were also visible in these shots, though they are not necessarily discernible when walking over the ground (Reyman 1989, 43–52).

Mound 5 (figure 7) yielded dozens of burials interred in a variety of positions. At least one was in a stone cist or slab-lined grave (Appendix A, figure A.1); others were partly flexed and either on their backs, on their sides, or on their chests with the heads turned to one side (figures A.3 to A.8). Note the lack of cultural debris around the skeletons. These are in burial mounds, *not* in house mounds or trash middens.[8] Pepper (1896a, 1896b) writes that it was his and Wetherill's practice to map the mounds and photograph each skeleton uncovered, but no maps are extant for these mounds, and the seven photographs reproduced here are the only ones I was able to find of the thirty to forty burials that they excavated from Mound 5.[9] They make it clear that few, if any, grave goods accompanied the interments, which offers support to both Pepper's (1896a, 1896b) and Wetherill's (1896) explanations of why they ceased digging in these mounds: they had little interest in excavating burials with few grave goods, as Pepper (1920, 347) also noted above for Mound 2. Furthermore, they make it clear that the skeletal materials were in generally poor condition except for the individuals designated N and 3 in Mound 5. Also note that there was apparently no consistent pattern in how the dead were laid to rest: flexed, on the back, on the chest, in a slab-lined or cist grave, and so on.

Whereas Pepper (1920, 339–51) states that they removed the "specimens" from Mound 1 and Mound 2 near Casa Rinconada (figure 19)—which may or may not have included the skeletal remains, as discussed earlier—neither his nor Wetherill's unpublished notes for Mound 5 or the other large mounds indicate that the skeletal materials were removed or that, if they were, they were kept as part of the Hyde Exploring Expedition collections. Pepper's unpublished notes for Mound 5 seem to indicate that the back dirt and poorly preserved skeletal materials were put into the arroyo, where subsequent flooding would have washed them away. As far as I can determine, the skeletal materials and any cultural items such as the slabs that lined the burial pit in figure A.1 were not kept and do not survive at the American Museum of Natural History, the Museum of the American Indian, Heye Foundation, the Field Museum of Natural History, the Peabody Museum, and other institutions.

These photographs are a visual record that can be used to make several important points: Mound 5 was large and high, and the burials shown are deep within the mound. Stratigraphic lines or lenses, especially in figure A.8, suggest that Mound 5 was built up or resurfaced over time, not unlike the situation found among burial mounds in the Eastern Woodlands; and *no* cultural debris appears to be present, thereby indicating that Mound 5 was neither a trash midden nor a house mound. The light-colored stratigraphic lenses might be ash that was scattered over the mound. Ash is important in Pueblo religion (Parsons 1939, passim; Stephen 1936, passim). During ceremonies, I have often seen ashes rubbed on individuals' heads as a purifying substance. Parsons (1932, 210, 432) notes the importance of ashes and ash piles at Isleta in conjunction with burial practices. Furthermore, the individual (skeleton 14) in Room 33 at Pueblo Bonito was laid on a bed of wood ashes atop a layer of yellow sand.

Once again, the question can be raised of why Pepper declined to publish the information on Mound 5 or the other large mounds that he and Wetherill excavated. He profiled the excavation of Mounds 1 and 2 in *Pueblo Bonito* (1920, 339–51), so why exclude the impressive Mound 5? No answer is forthcoming. Wetherill did not publish much in his lifetime (Wetherill 1894; McNitt 1966, 357), and his notes (1896) on the mound excavations were also unpublished.

Some of my readers, especially archaeologists, may question whether Mound 5 ever existed and where it is today, noting that the extensive survey during the multiple years of the Chaco Center's work in the canyon apparently did not record it. The Pepper–Wetherill unpublished photographs and notes, in my opinion, unquestionably demonstrate its previous existence. As to what happened to Mound 5, at the time Pepper and Wetherill excavated it in 1896 it was close to the arroyo's edge, and my best "guess" is that it eventually collapsed, as did several habitation structures such as "Arroyo House," also known as "Half House" (see Judd 1964, 31), along with the skeletal materials that Pepper and Wetherill *unfortunately, blatantly, and disrespectfully* threw into the arroyo at the end of their excavations. Kirk Bryan (1954, plate 5) shows two excellent examples of how the arroyo "ate" structures as its edge eroded and collapsed.

One last point needs to be repeated: The *best* evidence that these are burial mounds and not house mounds or trash mounds is *negative*. Were these either burial or trash mounds, one would expect to find cultural debris mixed in with the soil: ceramics, lithics, bits of textiles, pieces of sandals, wooden objects, floral debris, food remains including animal bones, and more. Except for the slabs used to enclose the human remains (cists) and the pottery interred with the skeletons—and, as noted, not much of that—there were *no* other cultural materials. These clearly were burial mounds and not house mounds or trash mounds.

CHAPTER FIVE

Summary and Conclusions

THERE IS A WEALTH of unpublished data on Pueblo Bonito and other Chacoan sites that is gradually being brought to the attention of archaeologists. Some data have been published in recent years, and more data are published here. Publication of the field notes, diaries, and photographs from the Hyde Exploring Expedition in their entirety would be invaluable to our understanding of Chacoan archaeology and the Ancestral Pueblo culture history of the canyon and its environs. These are primary data from work done from the late nineteenth through the first third of the twentieth century and cannot be replicated.

The most important unpublished data concern Chacoan burials, great house architecture, and painted ceramics. Although Clark Wissler wrote in his foreword to *Pueblo Bonito* that Pepper had published his field record in full, we have seen from the unpublished materials that both architectural details and room contents were not, and that important additional data are to be had that affect our understanding of the Hyde Exploring Expedition's work there. Additionally, substantial amounts of other significant data, such as the large numbers of finished turquoise beads, pendants, turquoise sets or tesserae, and small turquoise objects, plus a considerable quantity of turquoise in matrix, indicate that Pueblo Bonito served as a production center. Painted marks on certain Chacoan ceramic vessels suggest specialized production by specific potters (Fricke 1979). Various objects such as flutes, worked sandstone, basketry, and woven textiles painted using invested techniques, including pseudo-cloisonné, have not been reported in the published literature, although they are indicative of trade with Mesoamerican peoples. Until these unpublished primary data become generally available to archaeologists, our understanding of Chacoan archaeology and cultural history will continue to be limited and seriously flawed in many specific instances. Appendix C (below) on milkweed is an example of an unpublished minor floral specimen that might have significant implications for Chacoan collecting or the study of farming activities as well as ancient weaving. Furthermore, Pepper (1920, 68–69) briefly described a painted "altar cloth" and its removal from Room 13 at Pueblo Bonito, but he never published a photograph of it. Plates 4–5 are Pepper's unpublished, hand-colored photographs of the object in situ. The cloth is at the American Museum of Natural History and ought to be unwound, laid out, and studied in detail if possible.

Akins and Schelberg (1984, 92) state that more than 650 burials have been recovered from Chacoan sites that date from between AD 900 and 1300. In the most comprehensive compendium of Chaco burial data, Akins (1986, 7) notes that her discussion excludes data from the work of some of the earlier workers at Chaco Canyon, such as J. S, Newberry and John Wesley Powell, but cannot include their findings because the records apparently do not exist. Judd (1954, 325), citing personal communication from Col. D. K. B. Sellers of Albuquerque, writes that in the late 1890s when Richard Wetherill had his trading post nearby, Sellers and another man broke into "a large room on the west side of Bonito" and there found part of the "mummified" body of a woman and a quantity of turquoise, including two turquoise birds.

Again, no record of these finds remains other than Judd's brief account. If we use the 650+ figure as a base and add to it the unpublished data, such as the forty or so skeletons recovered by Pepper and Wetherill from a single trench in Mound 5 and then the dozens more from other mounds and sites they excavated but left unfinished and unreported, it is reasonable to suppose that the number of burials would exceed one thousand and very possibly be well over that. This is still not a huge number overall, but it possibly foreshadows a much larger number of burials yet to be discovered at Chaco. Therefore, to reiterate my earlier point, to the extent that current Chaco population estimates are based on the number of burials recovered, these estimates must be revised upward.

CHAPTER FIVE

Furthermore, as both Palkovich (1984) and Akins (1986) demonstrate, the reanalyses of existing collections such as Judd's (1954), made in the 1920s, show that many more individuals were interred than the original counts indicate. There are also earlier published accounts of Chacoan burials that may not have been counted by later scholars. One such example is Riley's (1954) brief report on a Chaco Canyon skeletal series from Bc-51, Bc-53, and Bc-59. One cannot determine whether the seventeen individuals are included in Akins's (1986) compendium; I think not because Akins does not cite the Riley publication. Once more, the number of burials from Chaco is significantly higher than many (most?) archaeologists think.

The numbers of burials are probably significantly higher still, and we now have the technological means to evaluate this hypothesis—to locate them in Chaco itself. As shown, both the published and unpublished literature on Chaco contains numerous references to cemeteries and mounds. I suggest using these references in conjunction with ground-penetrating radar and other remote sensing techniques to search the area west of Pueblo Pintado—and preferably on all sides of the site—for the large cemetery noted by Pepper (1920, 376) and where my field crews searched unsuccessfully in 1974 and 1976, the flats around Peñasco Blanco where Maher (1947) and later my field crews also searched unsuccessfully in 1974 and 1976, the area around Kin Bineola where Hrdlička (n.d.) located some seventy-two burials in 1899–1900 (see Akins 1986), the south side of Chaco toward the South Gap (Pepper 1896; Wetherill 1896) and south of it as well, and elsewhere. Assuming this research produces promising results, the finds must be verified by ground testing. Therein lies the rub: in this era of NAGPRA, the National Park Service is unlikely to issue a permit to conduct the fieldwork.

There must also be a revision upward of population estimates based on the number of hearths. Windes (1984, 77) states that he used a figure of forty-three hearths or fire pits for Pueblo Bonito, from which he derived a population of one hundred. However, as shown above, there were at least ninety-one hearths at Pueblo Bonito, which would effectively double Windes's population estimate. To the extent that hearths figure into it, the same sort of upward revision would apply to Bernardini's (1999) population estimate based on "residential units." More hearths equal more

PLATE 6

PLATES 6 and 7. 1896 hand-colored photographs of the "painted altar cloth" first uncovered in Room 13, Pueblo Bonito. *Photos*: George H. Pepper.

residential units, hence a greater population. Moreover, the architectural details in Pepper's unpublished field notes and diary might possibly change Bernardini's definition and understanding of the "residential units" and have additional implications for his population estimate. If we accept that there were at least ninety-one hearths rather than forty-three—a difference of forty-eight—and if, therefore, the number of residential units increases accordingly, and if we assume that each residential unit comprised a minimum of six people (Bernardini's estimate), then the population increases by 288 over Bernardini's (1999) seventy-person estimate to 358 persons, still much too low in my opinion, but five times Bernardini's number. Of course, the question of the contemporaneity of the hearths remains. However, in my opinion, I have no problem with my earlier estimate of one thousand (or more) inhabitants of Pueblo Bonito, and with a total population for Chaco Canyon at the height of its existence—from Peñasco Blanco to Pueblo Pintado—of three thousand people and maybe more based on my knowledge of the late precontact to early postcontact and modern pueblos such as Pecos, Gran Quivira, Taos, and Zuni.

Chaco Canyon and Pueblo Bonito, however, are not unique in this regard. As noted above, a wealth of unpublished primary data in all fields of anthropology is awaiting rediscovery and analyses. The Hyde Exploring Expedition, and separately Pepper and Wetherill, worked elsewhere in the Southwest, and much of the bounty of their efforts, revealed in the unpublished records, has yet to be studied and appreciated. There are also untapped sources of primary data in Ruins Stabilization Unit reports (see, e.g., Reyman 1978a; Vivian, et al. 1978) and in the papers of past archaeologists and other anthropological scholars. As I noted earlier, and previously (e.g., Reyman 1989), almost no archaeologists publish all their data. These materials are awaiting rediscovery, and the unpublished records can and will change our understanding of our subjects and their histories, just as the unpublished Pepper–Wetherill records have changed the archaeological history of Chaco Canyon and our understanding of the ancient Chacoans.

PLATE 7

APPENDIX A

IMAGES OF SKELETAL MATERIALS FROM PUEBLO BONITO AND THE PEPPER–WETHERILL MOUND 5, WSW OF PUEBLO DEL ARROYO

Notice: Readers are advised that these images are inherently sensitive and may be disturbing, even offensive to some. Care should be taken when viewing them.

APPENDIX A

APPENDIX A

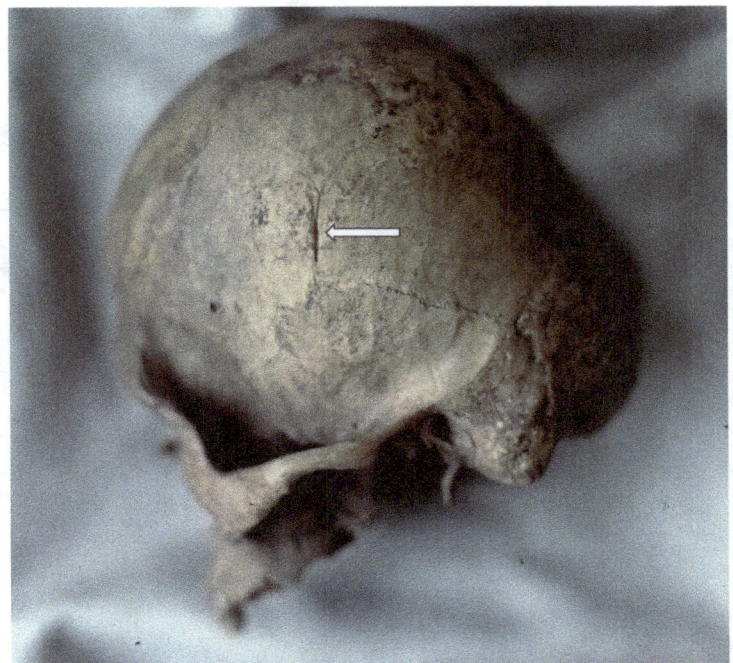

PLATE A-1. (*above*) Cranium H/3671 (Individual 13) from Room 33, showing cut mark on the lower left parietal bone marked by the arrow. *Photo*: Jonathan E. Reyman.

FIGURE A-1. (*opposite above*) 1896 Pepper–Wetherill photograph of a slab-lined or cist grave in Mound 5, west-southwest of Pueblo del Arroyo. Note the lack of cultural debris. The white pieces are bone. This is a burial mound, not a trash midden or house mound.

FIGURE A-2. (*opposite below*) "Burial Mound, Pueblo Bonito." Marietta Wetherill photograph #71,047 at the NPS Western Archaeological Center (given to Gordon Vivian) shows windblown debris atop a burial mound at Chaco Canyon. Despite the title, the actual location is not in or even next to Pueblo Bonito.

APPENDIX A

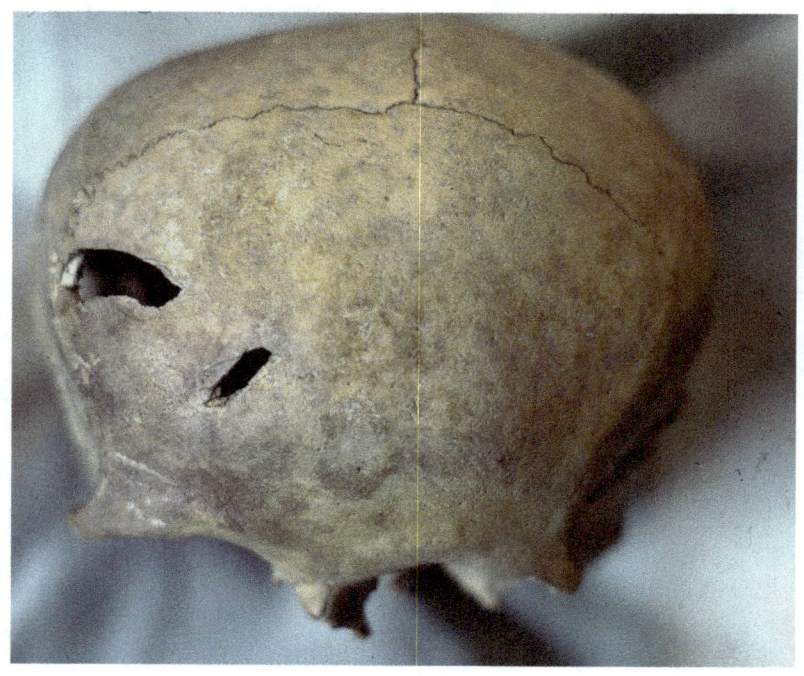

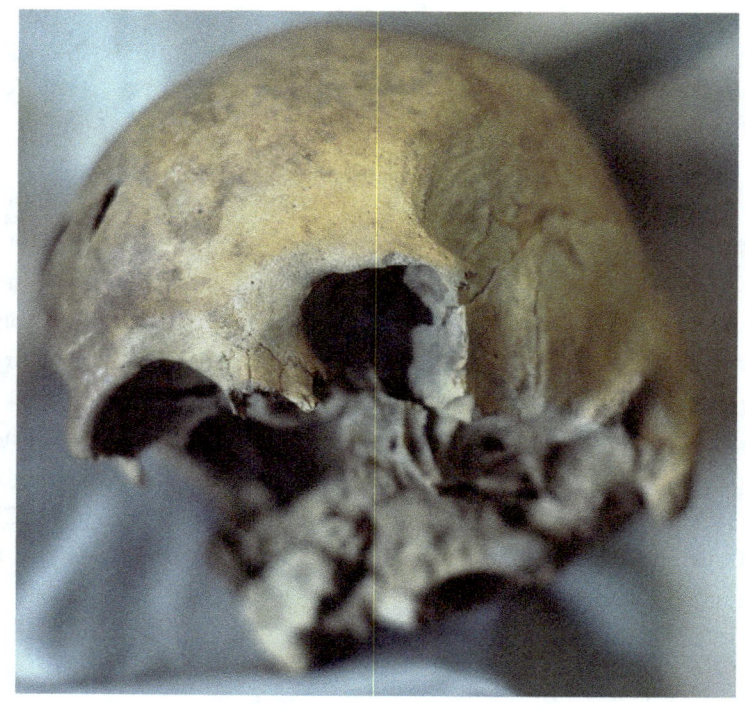

APPENDIX A

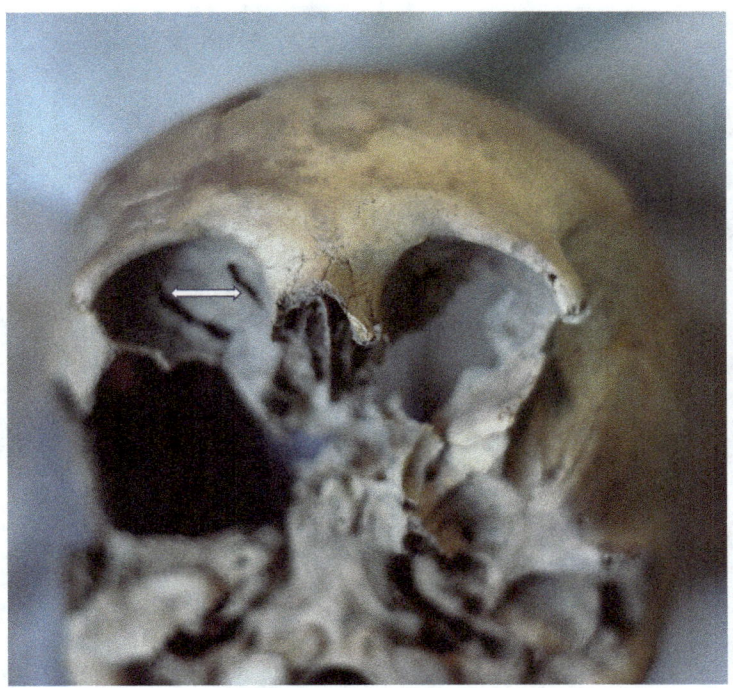

PLATE A-2. (*opposite above*) Cranium H/3672 (Individual 14) from Room 33, showing two puncture wounds through the right side. *Photo*: Jonathan E. Reyman.

PLATE A-3. (*opposite below*) Cranium H/3672 (Individual 14) from Room 33, showing the destruction of the face by one or more massive blows. The double-sided arrow points to the neurological infection noted by Nickels in Appendix B. *Photo*: Jonathan E. Reyman.

PLATE A-4. (*above*) Cranium H/3672 (Individual 14) from Room 33: a view from below of the destruction of the face by one or more massive blows. *Photo*: Jonathan E. Reyman.

APPENDIX A

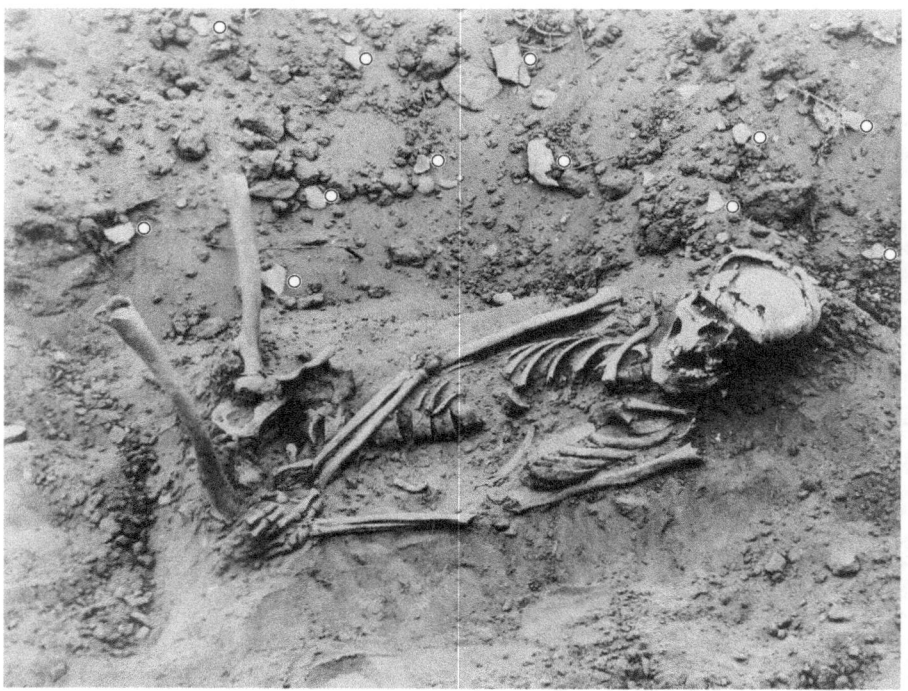

FIGURE A-3. (*above*) 1896 Pepper–Wetherill photograph of Burial 1 from Mound 5, west-southwest of Pueblo del Arroyo. The white "objects" marked with dots around the burial are bone fragments.

FIGURE A-4. (*opposite above*) 1896 Pepper–Wetherill photograph of Burial "N" (Individual 14) from Mound 5, west-southwest of Pueblo del Arroyo.

FIGURE A-5. (*opposite below*) 1896 Pepper–Wetherill photograph of Burial 4 from Mound 5, west-southwest of Pueblo del Arroyo. The dot marks a large skull fragment.

APPENDIX A

APPENDIX A

APPENDIX A

FIGURE A-6. (*opposite above*) 1896 Pepper–Wetherill photograph of Burial 5 from Mound 5, west-southwest of Pueblo del Arroyo, with contents in poor, fragmentary condition.

FIGURE A-7. (*opposite below*) 1896 Pepper–Wetherill photograph of Burial 2 from Mound 5, west-southwest of Pueblo del Arroyo.

FIGURE A-8. (*above*) 1896 Pepper–Wetherill photograph of Burial 3 from Mound 5, west-southwest of Pueblo del Arroyo, with stratigraphic lenses in the mound clearly visible.

APPENDIX B

OSTEOMETRIC DATA AND ANALYSIS OF THE SKELETAL MATERIALS IN PUEBLO BONITO ROOMS 32–33

MARTIN K. NICKELS, EDITED BY JONATHAN E. REYMAN

THE SKELETAL MATERIAL: EXCAVATION AND DISPOSITION

George Pepper's 1909 report on the excavations of Rooms 32 and 33 at Pueblo Bonito that he conducted in 1896 dealt extensively with the wealth of artifacts recovered, but he paid virtually no attention to the human skeletal remains also recovered there. Indeed, of the reported fifteen individuals excavated from these two rooms he wrote that "the burials furnish but meager data for study" (Pepper 1909, 249). Pepper's dismissal of the importance of these skeletal remains for understanding the nature of this unusual Puebloan burial complex is reflected in his method of assigning museum accession numbers to the bones: The two individuals found beneath a carefully constructed wooden plank flooring in Room 33 were given individual numbers (H/3671 and H/3672), and the skulls found in the upper fill of Room 33 were all assigned separate numbers (H/3659 to H/3670); but all of the postcranial remains from Room 33, as well as the headless Room 32 individual, were assigned a single accession number (H/3658), with no effort made to keep individual burials separate from one another. In the summer of 1980, all of these bones designated H/3658 were stored in specimen drawers by bone type at the American Museum of Natural History in New York. With the exception of the individual from Room 32, it proved impossible to associate any specific postcranial remains marked H/3658 with any of the eleven remaining skulls from the Room 33 fill. Some effort was made to affiliate the long bones of the legs with one another, but this did not prove to be satisfactory.

APPENDIX B

Pepper accurately described the individual in Room 32 so that the skeleton was recognizable in the American Museum collections. The following is taken from Pepper's actual unpublished field notes:

> The vertebrae were almost in a longitudinal plane—ten vertebrae were intact and in position as were also the sacrum and two pelvis bones. The other vertebra [sic] (3) fell when the man was removing the surface dirt and they too were probably in place. The vertebrae that were in place are numbered and run from 1 to 10—being numbered consecutively according to position.

These ten vertebrae were in articulation with the pelvis that Pepper recovered in Room 32. Other bones that Pepper recovered from Room 32 included an unknown number of ribs, a right clavicle, a left femur, and an unsided scapula. None of these bones nor any of the other three vertebrae mentioned by Pepper above could be positively identified in the Museum collections, although we did make efforts to do so.

It is also apparent that not all of the skeletal materials originally excavated and recovered by Pepper are present today in the collections of the American Museum. One specimen's disposition—skull H/3667—is clearly recorded, however. In an effort to locate missing specimens, we studied the museum's old accessions catalogues. A notation in the margin of one of the catalogues indicated that this particular specimen had been "exchanged" with Dr. Robert Broom of South Africa in 1914. There is no record of this skull ever having been studied, nor have we been successful in two efforts to locate this specimen in South Africa. Consequently, we had only eleven of the original twelve skulls found above the wooden plank floor in Room 33 to examine and study.

Further definite evidence that all of the skeletal remains originally recovered by Pepper are no longer together is the fact that one of the two burials (Number 13 or H/3671) that he found beneath the wooden plank floor in Room 33 is missing its pelvis. Pepper's field notes indicate that the pelvis (presumably meaning both innominates and the sacrum) of this individual was recovered. However, the pelvis is not present in the museum's collection today, and there is no record of its present whereabouts. It is impossible to determine whether the pelvis was "exchanged" with some scholar or institution (as in the case of the skull H/3667) or removed for some other purpose.

Still another complication is that there are only eleven pelves from the Room 33 fill, and it is not clear from either Pepper's original field notes or his publications whether a twelfth pelvis was ever recovered or whether, having been recovered, it has also been removed from the museum's collection. While we could find no record of such a removal, the combination of the length of time that has elapsed since the bones were first accessioned in 1896, the lumping of all the hundreds of postcranial remains removed from the fill of Room 33 under a single accession number, and Pepper's dismissal of the importance of these bones to his own studies does raise the possibility that a pelvis was removed and not returned. One distinct possibility is that more skeletal material than skull H/3667 was included in the "exchange" with Dr. Broom in 1914. We shall probably never know for sure.

METHODS OF SKELETAL ANALYSIS

A total of twenty different measurements were taken on the thirteen skulls and mandibles available for study. Eight indices were computed from these measurements. The cranial measurements and indices used are listed in table B.1. Another fourteen measurements were attempted on the postcranial material, but this proved a largely fruitless undertaking because meaningful data were obtainable for only two of the thirteen individuals.

The sex of the pelves and skulls were determined by evaluating a variety of morphological attributes. For the pelves, such attributes included the width of the greater sciatic notch, the shape of the body of the pubis, the presence or absence of the ventral arc, the medial aspect of the ischio-pubic ramus, the angle of the subpubic concavity, the presence or absence of scars of parturition, and the height of the isiac articular surface. Cranial sexing criteria included overall size, slope and height of the forehead, robusticity and rugosity of muscle attachment sites, and overall appearance of the mandible, including chin form and the gonial angle. Interpretations of the appearance of these various criteria were based on descriptions found in Bass (1971), Brothwell (1972), El-Najjar and McWilliams (1978), Stewart (1979a), and Ubelaker (1978). While it is always preferable to emphasize the importance of pelvic criteria over cranial criteria when determining the sex of an individual, this proved to be impossible in this instance for all of the individuals, with the exception of one of the two complete skeletons (Number 14) found by Pepper beneath the wood planking in Room 33. In no other instances was it possible to associate a particular pelvis with a specific skull. Consequently, pelvic sex determinations were made independently of cranial sex estimations, and this served to provide a check on the total number of males and females present as determined by the two separate skeletal regions (see below).

The age of the specimens was calculated by applying both the McKern and Stewart (1957) and Todd (1920) techniques to the public symphyseal surfaces of the pelves classified as males and the Gilbert and McKern (1973) pubic symphyseal stages to the pelves classified as females (table B.2). Age assessments of the skulls were based on dental eruption patterns and degree of sutural closure and obliteration. The fact that all of the skulls possessed completely erupted teeth with considerable wear and that the degree of cranial suture obliteration is useful only as a general indication of young, middle, or older adulthood, meant that age estimates based on the skull were of little value.

Table B.3 lists the incidence of nonmetric traits recorded. The skeletal landmarks and osteometric techniques utilized in mensuration can be found in Bass (1971), Brothwell (1972), and other common references on osteometry. Twenty-six cranial nonmetric traits were recorded. These are listed in the table. Definitions of these traits can be found in Brothwell (1972) and El-Najjar and McWilliams (1978).

NUMBER OF INDIVIDUALS

The problem of exactly how many individuals are represented by this skeletal collection is one we did not anticipate. Pepper thought that one individual was buried in Room 32 near the doorway of Room 33 and that there were twelve individuals present in the fill of Room 33 itself above the wooden plank floor. Finally, there were the two individuals he found beneath the wooden floor in Room 33. This represents a total of fifteen individuals. While the two individuals beneath the floor are well represented by relatively complete skeletons, there is some uncertainty about the actual number of individuals represented in the fill of Room 33 and in Room 32 (cf. Akins 2003, 96).

One of the twelve skulls that Pepper recovered in Room 33 is certainly missing and we do not know if a twelfth pelvis was recovered at all. If it was, but has since been removed from the collection, then we should have a total of twelve individuals from the fill of Room 33. The problem, of course, is that we do not have an accurate record of the number of pelves (or any other bones, for that matter) that Pepper recovered from this portion of Room 33.

There is another possibility, however: that the pelvis (and partially complete vertebral column) that Pepper unearthed in Room 32 at the doorway into Room 33 represent the "missing" twelfth pelvis from Room 33. If this is the case, then there would be only a total of twelve individuals buried above the level of the two found below the wooden floor in Room 33. It is not possible to rule out this possibility because a count of twenty of the most numerous bone specimens all catalogued as H/3658 failed to produce a total of more than twelve individuals. Because the H/3658 accession number includes the Room 32 material, as well as the material from the fill of Room 33, there may well be a total of only twelve individuals represented from both rooms, apart from the two found beneath the wooden floor, of course. This number would conflict with Pepper's conclusion that there was one individual in Room 32 and twelve in the fill of Room 33, for a total of thirteen (again, cf. Akins 2003, 96).

Further complicating this issue is the fact that even though Pepper recorded the recovery of a right clavicle, a left femur, a scapula (unsided), an unspecified number of ribs, three vertebrae in addition to the ten found in situ, and a single tooth in Room 32, these could not be positively separated from similar bones found in Room 33, all of which were designated H/3658. So while Pepper may be right in his conclusion that there were thirteen individuals, we are unable to verify that number from a count of the bones available to us for study. It must always be borne in mind that we know some bones are definitely missing from the collection—although even their presence would not necessarily increase the known number of individuals represented here—and it is possible that others are missing as well. If so, then there may well have been thirteen (or even more) individuals originally. There is simply no way to know for sure.

SEX AND AGE OF THE SPECIMENS

Of the eleven skulls found in the fill of Room 33 that were available for this study, six were classified as females and five were classified as males. But, as has already been noted above, sex determinations from cranial features are not the most dependable and should be considered less significant than assessments from the pelvis of the same individual. The disposition of the skeletal remains in this study, however, did not permit skull and pelvic associations to be made. What was possible was to make independent sex determinations of the eleven pelves from the Room 33 fill and to use these assessments as a check on the sex determinations made from the skulls. These eleven pelves also represent six females and five males. In addition, the Room 32 pelvis is that of a male.

Both of the individuals found beneath the wooden flooring in Room 33 are also males. Skeleton number 13 is missing the pelvis as previously noted but was classified as a male from an assessment of cranial features. Skeleton number 14 was classified as a male on the basis of both pelvic and cranial features.

Still a further check on the number of males and females represented in the H/3658 collection was provided by measuring the diameters of the femoral heads and then classifying them according to the scale developed by Karl Pearson in 1919 and reproduced in Bass (1971, 173). This classification is based on size, with those femoral heads larger than about 45 mm being classified as males and those smaller than about 41 mm being classified as females. On this basis, five of the ten measurable left femora would be males and five would be females, with a clear dichotomy of 5 mm existing between the sexes. Of the nine right femora with measurable heads, five are males and four are females, with a 4 mm dichotomy between the sexes. While this may not be the most dependable of sexing criteria, the very even distribution of males and females in this particular collection may be seen as being supportive of the more reliable pelvis-based sexual classifications. All three measurable femoral heads from the two burials beneath the Room 33 flooring had diameters in excess of 45 mm and are considered male by Pearson's criteria. These classifications are also in agreement with the assigned sex based on both the pelvic and cranial assessments of the two individuals. The essentially even distribution of males and females in the burials recovered from the fill in Room 33 is extremely significant and its implications will be discussed later.

As noted above, pubic symphyseal ages of the pelves from Rooms 32–33 are listed in table B.2. The letter designations refer to either penciled or ink identification markings on the pelves that were already present prior to our arrival and study at the museum. The McKern and Stewart (1957) and Todd (1920) methods were both applied to the male pelves as a check on each other and because of recent studies suggesting that the McKern–Stewart system is more dependable before thirty years of age and the Todd system after thirty years of age (Stewart 1979a, 163). For the female pelves, the Gilbert and McKern method was used, although with some hesitancy because of criticisms of its reliability and accuracy (Suchey 1979).

The majority of the pelvic age assessments seem to fall in the thirty-to-fifty-year age range, with only one specimen (F) being significantly younger, at about twenty-three years of age.

METRIC ANALYSIS: CRANIAL

Table B.1 lists the actual cranial measurements of the thirteen skulls available for analysis in this collection and also lists the cranial indices calculated for the specimens. All of the specimens manifest the lambdoidal flattening characteristic of contemporary prehistoric Southwestern skeletal series (Bennett 1975; Hooton 1930). That such artificial cranial deformation exists in these specimens should be borne in mind when comparing them to other skeletal series.

In terms of the classification of the various indices of the skull, these individuals are all hyperbrachycranic, or very broad-headed. Such indices are typical for crania manifesting artificial lambdoidal flattening. The specimens are also high-headed in terms of the length-height index, again the result of the artificial cranial deformation. As a group, the specimens are all leptenic (upper facial index) and leptoprosopic (total facial index): that is, slender or narrow-faced. The females are more medium-faced and the males more narrow-faced, however, when broken down by sex. As a group, the specimens are all mesorrhine or medium-nosed, which is also true for just the females, but the males are slightly narrow-nosed. Finally, specimens of both sexes have relatively narrow eye orbits (hypsiconchy).

STATURE

Stature reconstructions were made using the femora. Since these bones cannot be associated clearly with any of the skulls or pelves—with the exception of Burials 13 (H/3671) and 14 (H/3672)—the assignment of sex was based on femoral head diameters. Using the Pearson criteria cited above, five pairs of measurable femora were classified as male: specimens A, B, C, D, and E. Five other measurable pairs of femora were classified as females: specimens G, H, I, J, and L. Stature estimations were calculated separately for these two groups and burials 13 and 14. The regression formulae of Santiago Genoves (1967) were used in the calculations. Stature estimates for the males ranged from 162.98 cm to 171.34 cm, with an average of 165.92 cm (about 5 feet, 5 inches). Stature estimates for the females ranged from 153.95 cm to 156.93 cm, with an average of 155.53 cm (about 5 feet, 1 inch). Burial 13 has an estimated stature of 168.52 cm (about 5 feet, 6 inches), while Burial 14 has an estimated stature of 165.13 cm (about 5 feet, 5 inches).

PATHOLOGIES

George Pepper's (1909, 1920) description of the skeletal remains from Room 33 as being scattered and in disarray led us to consider the possibility that these individuals were deliberately dismembered following their death. Pepper concluded that the skeletal scatter was the result of postmortem water disturbance in the room. We decided that there was the possibility that the bodies had been deliberately dismembered and/ or scattered following death. Consequently, we looked for cutting marks (Stewart 1979a, 33–35) on the ends of long bones, around the back and base of the cranium, the mandibular condyles, and the cervical vertebrae. No such marks were found. We found no evidence whatsoever of deliberate dismemberment or mutilation.

Several specimens showed evidence of extensive tooth wear, tooth loss, and alveolar resorption. At least four specimens (H/3659, H/3660, H/3669, and H/3672) show extensive wear on one or both mandibular condyles, reflecting tempero-mandibular stress while chewing. Three specimens (H/3660, H/3661, and H/3672) possess slightly broken nasal bones, indicative of pre-mortem trauma. There is one instance of bilateral cribra orbitalia in specimen H/3665. The manifestation is very slight.

Without question, specimen H/3672 (one of the two crypt burials) is the most fascinating in regard to the amount and variety of pathological and traumatic conditions. Appendix A, plate A.4 shows several lesions on the internal surface of the upper cranial vault. The individual clearly suffered from some kind of neurological infection. Plate A.2 shows two puncture wounds in the right supraorbital area. The larger one measures approximately 35 mm by 10 mm, while the smaller one is approximately 17 mm long and 4 mm wide. Both openings extend completely through the frontal bone. There is no evidence of healing or bone repair along the edges of either puncture. The lack of healing indicates that the wounds occurred shortly prior to death, and it is highly unlikely that they were self-administered. The most reasonable conclusion is that the individual died from these head wounds that almost certainly penetrated the brain and that the blows producing the puncture wounds were deliberately administered. As noted earlier, his face was also bashed in, although this could have occurred after the puncture wounds to the skull had already killed him.

COMPARISONS TO OTHER SERIES

Tables B.3 and B.4 present some comparative statistics of cranial and mandibular measurements for the Rooms 32–33 skeletal specimens and three other prehistoric Southwestern skeletal series. Table B.3 presents nonmetric data. Both the Point of Pines and Casas Grandes specimens used are from approximately the same time period as are these Pueblo Bonito burials. The Middle Population specimens from Point of Pines date from about AD 1000 to 1285 (Bennett 1975). The combined Medio I and II population from Casas Grandes dates from approximately AD 1050 to 1340 (Butler 1971).[1] Additional metric comparative data were used from other (undated) Chaco Canyon specimens recorded by Hrdlička (1931) and nonmetric data recorded by Corruccini (1972).

No formal statistical tests were performed for this descriptive study of the Rooms 32–33 skeletons for two reasons. First, only grouped data were available from the Point of Pines and Casas Grandes specimens, precluding statistical tests. Second, it was decided to limit this work to the combined descriptive analysis of the artifactual and skeletal material because they have never appeared together, despite the fact that the excavations were concluded some 113 years ago.

In terms of the metric data, the Rooms 32–33 individuals are both broader-headed and larger-faced than the other series. This is the case for both sexes. Female stature is 4.8 cm taller than that reported by Bennett (1975) for the Middle Population from Point of Pines and about one-half of a centimeter shorter than that reported by Butler (1971) for the combined Medio I and II population from Casas Grandes. Male stature of the Rooms 32–33 individuals is about 6.5 cm taller than that reported for the Middle Population males from Point of Pines. It is about 2.8 cm taller than that reported for the Medio I and II period males from Casas Grandes. Burial 13 is 9.1 cm taller than the Point of Pines male average and about 5 cm taller than the Casas Grandes male average. Burial 14 is about 5.7 cm taller than the Point of Pines average and about 2 cm taller than the Casas Grandes average. From these figures, it is clear that the Pueblo Bonito individuals from Rooms 32–33 are as tall or taller than those from two temporally related sites.

In terms of the nonmetric attributes recorded, it is difficult to generalize because of the numerous gaps in the comparative data from the other three series. However, there does not appear to be any pattern of note.

APPENDIX B

SUMMARY

In sum, the results of our study of the human skeletal remains from Rooms 32 and 33 at Pueblo Bonito include the following:

- Based on assessments of the pelves, skulls, and femora, there are five middle to older adult females and five predominantly middle to older adult males represented by the skeletal remains found in the fill of Room 33. (One of the five males is a young adult of approximately twenty-three years of age.)
- Based on an assessment of the pelvis, the individual found in Room 32 near the doorway to Room 33 is a middle-aged adult male.
- Based on an assessment of the skull and the femur, skeleton 13 (H/3671), found buried beneath the wooden plank flooring of Room 33, is that of an adult male.
- Based on assessments of the pelvis, skull, and femur, skeleton 14 (H/3672) is that of an older adult male who apparently died from two puncture wounds to the right frontal area of the skull (and possibly from a massive blow to his face).
- Stature of the Room 33 females averaged almost 157 cm (or about 5 feet, 1 inch). Stature of the Room 33 males averaged nearly 166 cm (or about 5 feet, 5 inches). Individual 13 stood about 168.5 cm (about 5 feet, 6 inches) tall, and individual 14 stood about 165 cm (about 5 feet, 5 inches) tall.
- Aside from the cut marks to the skull of individual 13 (Appendix A, plate A.1), and the cut marks on the left femur and the puncture wounds and extensive frontal damage to the skull of individual 14, there is no evidence of deliberately inflicted injuries, mutilations, or dismemberment in the remaining skeletal material from these two rooms.
- On the basis of only limited statistical comparisons, the Rooms 32–33 individuals appear to be broader headed and larger-faced than roughly contemporaneous series from Casas Grandes and Point of Pines, as well as other (undated) Chaco Canyon specimens.

Table B.1. Individual Skull Measurements (in mm)

SKULL #	3659	3660	3661	3662	3663	3664	3665	3666	3668	3669	3670	3671	3672
SEX	F	F	M	M	F	M	F	F	F	M	M	M	M
CRANIUM													
Maximum Length	168	157	160	161	156	176	146	173	NA	169	176	159	163
Maximum Breadth	167	161	152	164	157	153	166	149	NA	159	165	163	155
Basion–Bregma	144	150	143	147	147	150	146	140	NA	146	138	144	151
Endobasion–Nasion	100	93	96	101	97	102	07	115	NA	103	102	99	99
Endobasion–Gnathion	111	98	115	110	99	112	104	118	NA	Na	127	NA	NA
Minimum Frontal	109	98	93	94	97	97	93	93	NA	93	101	94	98
Bizygomatic	138	136	131	144	138	139	135	131	NA	136	143	147	NA
Nasion–Alveolar	76	70	76	83	72	81	75	(71)	NA	78	81	78	NA
Nasion–Gnathion	122	110	126	121	124	137	120	121	NA	NA	133	NA	NA
Nasal Height	54	50	55	55	51	56	52	50	NA	57	55	54	NA
Nasal Breadth	27	26	28	26	25	25	24	26	NA	25	27	28	NA
Left Orbital Height	36	35	34	36	36	35	36	35	NA	35	35	35	NA
Left Orbital Breadth	39	38	36	40	38	36	38	37	NA	41	37	39	NA
Interorbital Breadth	28	27	27	23	26	24	24	24	NA	22	28	24	NA
MANDIBLE													
Bigonial Diameter	97	101	102	104	102	104	100	97	100	108	103	101	106
Height–Ascending Ramus	64	64	73	66	60	70	53	67	65	62	71	50	66
Bicondylar Width	119	122	120	125	128	125	108	123	121	126	126	130	129
Length	108	99	105	104	103	115	105	106	104	NA	113	106	109
Symphyseal Height	35	(35)	35	(30)	36	38	36	36	37	(32)	39	(35)	35
INDICES													
Cranial Index	99.40	102.55	95.00	101.86	100.64	86.93	113.70	86.13	NA	94.08	93.75	102.52	95.09
Cranial Module	158.67	156.00	151.67	157.33	153.33	159.67	152.67	154.00	NA	158.00	159.67	155.33	156.30
Length–Height	85.71	(95.54)	89.33	91.30	94.23	85.23	100.00	80.92	NA	86.39	78.41	90.57	92.60
Breadth–Height	86.23	93.17	94.08	89.63	93.63	98.04	87.95	93.96	NA	91.82	83.64	88.34	97.40
Upper Facial	55.07	51.47	58.02	57.64	52.17	58.27	55.56	(54.20)	NA	(57.35)	56.64	(53.06)	NA
Total Facial	88.41	80.88	96.13	84.03	89.86	98.56	88.89	92.37	NA	NA	93.09	NA	NA
Nasal	50.00	52.00	50.91	47.27	49.02	44.64	46.15	52.00	NA	43.86	49.09	61.85	NA
Orbital	92.31	92.11	94.44	90.00	94.74	97.22	92.11	94.59	NA	85.37	94.59	89.74	NA

Martin K. Nickels 1981.

NA = Not available due to bone destruction or alveolar resorption

( ) = Incomplete measurement

Table B.2. Pubic Symphyseal Age Assessments

MALE SPECIMENS	MCKERN-STEWART AGE (YEARS)	TODD AGE (YEARS)
3658 A (pencil)	36+ ($\bar{x}$=41)	45–50
3658 B (pencil)	29+ ($\bar{x}$=35.84)	39–44
3658 C (pencil)	36+ ($\bar{x}$=41)	45–50
3658 D (pencil)	29+ ($\bar{x}$=35.84)	39–44
3658 E (pencil—Room 32)	29+ ($\bar{x}$=35.84)	39–44
3658 F (pencil)	18–23 ($\bar{x}$=20.89)	22–24
3671 (pencil)	Not given	Not given
3672 (pencil)	29+ ($\bar{x}$=35.84)	39–44
FEMALE SPECIMENS	**GILBERT-MCKERN AGE (YEARS)**	
3658 G (pencil)	44–54 ($\bar{x}$=47.75)	
3658 H (pencil)	30–47 ($\bar{x}$=36.90)	
3658 A (ink)	23–39 ($\bar{x}$=32)	
3658 B (ink)	30–47 ($\bar{x}$=36.90)	
3658 C (ink)	Too worn for calculation	
3658 D (ink)	Too worn for calculation	

Martin K. Nickels, 1981.

McKern-Stewart and Gilbert-McKern ages provided by mean and mean/average ($\bar{x}$)

Todd age not provided for females

Table B.3. Comparative Non-Metric Traits Frequencies (in mm)

	THIS STUDY	MESA VERDE (BENNETT 1975)	POINT OF PINES (BENNETT 1975)	PUEBLO BONITO (CORRUCCINI 1972)	CASA GRANDES MEDIO I AND II (BUTLER 1971)
Inca Bone	.00	.18	.10		.03
Lamboid Ossicle	.46				
Asterionic Ossicle	.35				
Parietal Notch	.15				.69
Epipteric Bone	.04		.25		
Os Japonicum	.00				.00
Metopic Suture	.00	.00	.03		.004
Frontal Grooves	.27				
Supraorbital Foramen	.42				.38
Multiple Supraorbital Foramina	.04				.03
Supraorbital Notch	.54				.56
Trochlear Spurs	.00				
Accessory Infraorbital Foramina	.04			.23	.03
Palatine Torus	.31				.10
Maxillary Torus	.00				
Foramen of Huschke	.00			.23	
Tympanic Dehiscence	.27	.33	.31		
Auditory Exostoses	.00				.00
Pharyngeal Fossa	.00		.33	.27	N/A
Divided Hypoglossal Canal	.04				.08
Closed Postcondylar Foramen	.00				
Pterygo-Spinous Bridging	.00				
Mylohyoid Bridging	.00			.04	.07
Mandibular Torus	.00	.05	.009	.01	.15
Multiple Mental Foramina	.00				.02
Pterion Shape: Front-Temporal (K)	.00	.00	.00		
Pterion Shape: Parietal-Sphenoid (H)	100.00	100.00	100.00		

Martin K. Nickels, 1981.

Table B.4. Comparative Cranial Facial Metrics (in mm)

	THIS STUDY, M/F	MESA VERDE (BENNETT 1975), M/F	POINT OF PINES (BENNETT 1975), M/F	PUEBLO BONITO (CORRUCCINI 1972), M/F	CASA GRANDES, MEDIO I, M/F	CASA GRANDES, MEDIO II, M/F
Cranial Length	166.29/160	169.9/163.1	164.4/156.6	x/x*	168/160.2	169.6/162.1
Cranial Breadth	158.71/159.25	141.5/141.7	140.8/139.4	x/x*	138/131.7	140.8/135.6
Cranial Height	145.57/145.4	139.1/136.8	137.3/133.6	x/x*	151/131	x/140.2
Cranial Index	95.60/100.48	83.5/86.5	84.3/88.8	x/x*	x/x*	x/x*
Facial Height	129.25/119.4	120.2/107.7	117/107.8	x/x*	106/113	120.2/114.2
Bizygomatic	140/135.6	136.6/127.1	140.8/139.4	x/x*	x/132	138.6/121.8
Nasal Width	26.5/25.6	25.4/25.3	25/24.1	24.58/24.92	22/25.3	24.7/26.1
Nasal Height	55.33/51.4	51.4/47.7	48/47.4	49.34/47.37	41/47.3	50.8/47.1
Nasal Index	47.94/49.83	49.42/53.03	52.08/50.84	49.82/52.6	53.66/53.49	48.62/55.41

Martin K. Nickels 1981.

* Sex could not be determined.

APPENDIX C

THE IDENTIFICATION AND SIGNIFICANCE OF A MILKWEED SEED

This brief discussion of milkweed is included to give readers an idea of the range of information available in the unpublished Pepper–Wetherill materials from Chaco Canyon. Due to the possible implications for Chaco farming practices and textile manufacture, the subject deserves greater treatment than is possible here.

Although a species of milkweed (*Asclepias macrotis* Torr.) is reported from Chaco Canyon (Cully 1985, 448), milkweed is rarely, if ever, mentioned in archaeological site reports for Chaco. Neither Pepper (1920) nor Judd (1954) note its presence either in raw form or in artifacts. Nevertheless, Pepper did recover milkweed pods and seeds from Pueblo Bonito, though he may not have known at the time that they were milkweed. Later he gave at least one seed to Matilda Coxe Stevenson at the Smithsonian Institution, apparently with a request that she have it identified.[1] Stevenson replied in a letter to Pepper in which she provided the identification, a sketch of the specimen (figure C.1), and some additional ethnographic information:

> I am enclosing a rough sketch of the seed you were good enough to give me when I last visited your museum. I remember that you had only a few seeds of this character. I am very anxious to learn just where the seed was found. I regret to confess that I have forgotten, if you told me. I would be very pleased to have a few lines from your pen to insert in the paper I will soon have ready for publication[2] . . . I know that the Zuni made sashes and other articles, of the milkweed, *Asclepias incarnata* Engelm, and they still spin it for certain religious purposes. Dr. [William] Rose classifies the specimen you gave me as *Asclepias involucrata* Engelm (Stevenson 1909).

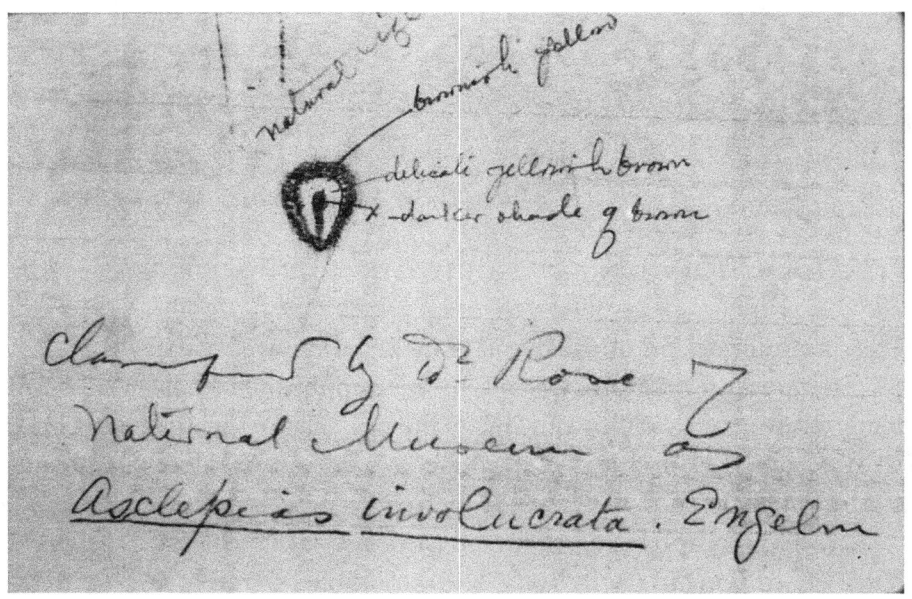

FIGURE C.1. Sketch by Matilda Coxe Stevenson of the Smithsonian of a milkweed seed sent to her for identification by George Pepper.

It is not known *why* Pepper wanted the seed identified, and he made no use of the data provided by Stevenson in *Pueblo Bonito* or any other publication. One possible consequence, however, of his not using her information is that Pepper mistakenly identified five textile fragments he found as woven from cotton (Pepper 1920, 106–7) when, in fact, they are woven from milkweed (Reyman 1992, 78). It is also possible that some of the cordage he excavated is made from milkweed.

There are at least three implications of the identification of milkweed. First, milkweed may have been more important at Chaco Canyon than is now thought. It would be worth reexamining the relatively few other textiles and the cordage to see whether they are, indeed, cotton, or whether some or all are made from milkweed.

Second, we know from the ethnographic literature that the Zuni used milkweed for food (Cushing 1920, 228, 561), as well as for the garments mentioned above by Stevenson. The Tewa also used milkweed for food and cordage, and as medicine (Robbins et al. 1916, 54). Again, it would be worth reexamining old artifact collections from Chaco (Pepper's, Judd's, Hewett's, etc.) to determine whether there are objects made from milkweed that were overlooked, unreported, or misidentified. Finally, if milkweed is, indeed, more common than now thought, it might have been cultivated and not simply collected, and this would be significant in terms of our understanding of ancient farming at Chaco Canyon.

APPENDIX D

RESEARCH RESOURCES

INSTITUTIONS VISITED

I visited some of these institutions, such as the AMNH, FMNH, Smithsonian, and Tulane, repeatedly over more than fifty years of research.

- American Museum of Natural History
- Aztec National Monument
- Chaco Culture National Historical Park
- Field Museum of Natural History
- Heye Foundation, Museum of the American Indian
- Heye Foundation, Museum of the American Indian, Bronx, NY Repository
- Laboratory of Anthropology Library, Santa Fe
- Latin American Library, Tulane University
- Maxwell Museum of Anthropology, University of New Mexico
- Middle American Research Institute, Tulane University
- Museum of Northern Arizona
- National Park Service, Western Archaeological Research Center
- New Orleans Museum of Art
- Peabody Museum, Harvard University
- Pennsylvania State University
- Philadelphia Art Museum
- Robert S. Peabody Institute of Archaeology, Phillips Academy, Andover, Massachusetts

- School of American Research (now School of Advanced Research)
- Smithsonian Institution
- Southwest Cultural Resources Center, University of New Mexico
- University of Pennsylvania Museum
- Wupatki National Monument

INSTITUTION CONSULTED

- Transvaal Museum, Pretoria, South Africa (now Ditsong National Museum of Natural History)

INDIVIDUALS CONSULTED

- Jeanette Cameron (George H. Pepper's daughter) and James Cameron (Jeanette Cameron's husband)
- Dorothy Keur (Jeanette Pepper Cameron's anthropology professor at the University of New Mexico)
- Homer Hastings (former Chaco Canyon superintendent)

NOTES

CHAPTER ONE

1. The Department of Anthropology register that we signed lists Akins's visit before ours. The results of her study are in Akins 1986, 135–41, 162–63.

CHAPTER TWO

1. Much of Luhrs' material, however, is included in later publications such as Mathien and Windes 1988; Reyman 1971, 269–70; and Vivian and Reiter 1960, 53–61).
2. The late C. Randall Morrison, the Chaco Park archaeologist, with whom I was friends for over fifty years, found wood, nails, and other debris when the park was doing roadwork in that area east of Pueblo Bonito. He exclaimed, "Oh my God, there's a historic site here!" The image I found of the first Wetherill store resolved the mystery.
3. As discussed later in this volume, Hewett's supposition was to some extent correct in that there were burial mounds in the rincon to the southeast of Casa Rinconada.
4. As I have discussed earlier (Reyman 1989, 44), Pepper did not publish all his data from the Hyde Exploring Expedition fieldwork at Chaco Canyon, so Judd seems to have been unaware that Pepper found more burials in the general area around Casa Rinconada than just those belonging to local house groups.
5. This was not exactly true when Judd wrote it and is less so today. For example, Kidder (1924, 33) wrote of his work at Pecos, "We have already taken out some twelve hundred skeletons, and have as yet barely scratched the cemeteries." By Kidder's own estimate (31), his work cleared only about 12 to 15 percent of the site (cf. Hooton 1930; Marden 2011, 298 notes 1,938 individuals recovered). More than 150 individuals were unearthed

at the Pueblo III site of Salmon Ruins (Shipman 2006, 327–28; Espinosa 2006, 332). About 550 came from Mound 7 at Gran Quivira, and Hayes et al. (1981, 169) noted that an equal number were probably yet undiscovered. By 1979, when excavation of burials at Grasshopper Pueblo was halted, some 700 inhumations had been discovered at the site (Reid and Whittlesey (1999, x), and more than 150 individuals were found at Arroyo Hondo (Palkovich 1980, 1, 3). Admittedly, Gran Quivira (Las Humanas) and Grasshopper Pueblo (Mogollon) were not Pueblo III sites, and Arroyo Hondo was founded late in the period (ca. AD 1300). The point is that significant numbers of burials have been found at some large sites, though the paucity of burials in Pueblo III Chacoan sites (and at Pueblo III Mesa Verde sites and elsewhere) appears to be the norm.

6. I have previously suggested (Reyman 1989, 51) the possibility that Richard Wetherill is buried in an earlier Chacoan burial mound among the people he once studied, in the cemetery his wife, Marietta, later created just west of Pueblo Bonito (plates 6–7; Marietta Wetherill was buried there alongside him in 1948). It was also used to inter Navajo individuals who resided in Chaco Canyon and its close environs. It is clear, if one visits the site, that the cemetery is located on a raised or elevated area. If I am correct in my supposition that the Wetherill gravesite was once used by the ancient Bonitans to bury their dead, then judging by the size of it, it could contain many dozens of interments. And it would be a cemetery in close proximity to a major site.

    Despite Judd's comment about there being nothing to indicate burial in the talus at the base of the north cliff (1954, 341), one wonders whether the ancient Bonitans previously used the area for internments. By contrast, Hewett (1936a, 118) notes that two or three burials came from the talus area behind Chetro Ketl. It is worth pointing out that Pepper (1899b) refers to such burial mounds on the talus as being "simply the soil that has washed down from the mesa and formed a deposit, from two to three feet in depth, on the rocky slope below: it was here that the skeletons were found." However, testing for burials in the talus presents obvious problems, not the least of which is getting beneath the rock fall that has occurred during the past eight hundred to nine hundred years.

7. Pepper and Wetherill actually excavated forty-nine burials from Pueblo

Bonito and the small sites mentioned by Hewett, plus partial remains of another fifteen individuals (Pepper 1920, 339–51; cf. Akins 1986, 9). However, many more were recorded in their unpublished field records, as discussed later in this paper.

8. The late J. Charles Kelley, one of my major advisors and later colleague, suggested the term "Great Sanctuary" during discussions about my dissertation (Reyman 1971). Following Kelley, I prefer the term Great Sanctuary to Great Kiva because Great Kiva implies a similar function to a kiva, albeit on a much larger scale, whereas I think the two types of structures had quite distinct functions or purposes. A Great Sanctuary was a communal structure used for ritual events intended to bind together the people of the great house, similar to the Zuni *Sha'lako* ceremony held each December. By contrast, kivas are society or clan structures, and while community members other than those who belong to the clan or society may, in some instances, attend ceremonies held within, kiva ceremonies are primarily "members only" events. Note that Hewett (1936, 68, 78) was probably the first to suggest the term "Greater Sanctuaries."

9. Having worked at Chaco Canyon for a number of years, I would not want to be at the bottom of a trench eighteen feet deep and three feet wide. At Pueblo Bonito and elsewhere at Chaco, walls and ceilings did, in fact, collapse on several occasions during the Hyde Exploring Expedition work, though no one was killed or seriously injured.

10. See the site at http://www.chacoarchive.org.

11. I originally incorporated into the text of this book the 1896 Pepper–Wetherill photographs of burials, my American Museum of Natural History photographs of Pepper's collection of crania and other skeletal remains from Rooms 32–33 at Pueblo Bonito, and the crania excavated by Moorehead that are now in the Peabody Museum (Harvard). It was never my intent for these to offend readers. However, at the suggestion of Joe Watkins, who reviewed the manuscript, I reduced the number of images, deleted the three Moorehead photographs, moved the images to Appendix A, and inserted an advisory warning immediately under the appendix title that the images may be offensive to some readers. I also reduced the printed size of the images by 50 percent to lessen, to some extent, their visual impact on first viewing. Finally, I changed the book's title to eliminate the word "burials."

CHAPTER THREE

1. Pepper was probably already ill with the first signs of the kidney disease that would kill him prematurely in 1924, at age 51. He died of nephritis that may have started to develop during his time at Chaco Canyon. Wetherill had dug a well, and the water it produced was alkaline, even after it was filtered through cotton batting to "purify" it. It was used for drinking and in coffee. Pepper's 1896a, 1896b, and 1897 unpublished materials note the presence of small "pebbles" in the abdominal area of a number of skeletons. Pepper did not collect these pebbles, but they may have been kidney stones due to the alkaline water in ancient Chaco Canyon.

2. According to a June 1, 1981 letter to me from photo librarian Susan Harris of the National Park Service's Western Archaeological Research Center, this is Photograph 71,047 in their archive, and the note with it reads, "Burial Mound, Pueblo Bonito: In many places the ground is thickly strewn with human bones and pottery. The wind having blown the light material (sand and ashes) of the mounds away leaving hundreds of skulls and bones sometimes covering acres in extent. The mounds in places are yet 20 to 30 feet high."

3. There were inconsistencies in the measurement systems used: metrics in some cases, English feet and inches in others.

4. Akins (1986, 164; table B.1.) indicates that Mound 2, from which Pepper (1920, 341–51) reports skeletons 12–30, was site Bc-117, Bc-118, or 29SJ383. She does not state the basis for this. In my opinion, the lack of definite correspondence leaves open the question of whether Burial Mound 2 was none of these three sites but was, in fact, a separate burial mound and not a house mound or trash midden as Akins (1986, 15) suggests.

5. Walls and ceilings did, in fact, collapse on several occasions during the Hyde Exploring Expedition work at Pueblo Bonito and elsewhere at Chaco, though no one was killed or seriously injured.

6. The wood planks that comprised this floor apparently no longer exist, and there is no extant record at the American Museum of Natural History or the former Museum of the American Indian that the planks were ever entered into their inventories for Pueblo Bonito. I did hear from an older collections assistant at the AMNH that the planks became dried out, warped badly, deteriorated, and had long ago been discarded. It must also be noted that Akins (2003, 96) states that there were as many as

the remains of sixteen disarticulated individuals above the plank floor, including fourteen by "fibula counts," rather than the twelve first noted by Pepper. Nickels and I did not obtain a similar count to Akins when we studied the skeletal materials at the American Museum of Natural History (see Appendix B, below).

7. Pueblo Bonito cylinder jars have recently received a great deal of attention and analysis (see Crown and Hurst 2009, Crown 2020) because of their apparent ceremonial use linked with the consumption of a cacao drink and as one more of many indications of Ancestral Puebloan ties to Mesoamerica. Earlier, Fricke (1979) demonstrated by studying painted motifs and also marks on the lower portions of the jars extending onto their bottoms that the jars were made in pairs. Crown thinks they were made in pairs or in groups of four based on the same criteria.

8. Many more Mesoamerican and Mesoamerican-influenced materials were found at Pueblo Bonito (and other great houses such as Chetro Ketl and Pueblo del Arroyo), e.g., the remains of thirty-one Scarlet macaws (*Ara macao*), pseudo-cloisonné invested wood objects, sandstone, basketry, gourd rinds, a textile, and, notably the basalt mortar from Room 80 (Pepper 1920, 264–67); copper bells, a conch-shell trumpet, and fragments of strombus shells in Room 13 (P69); a murex shell trumpet and four murex shell fragments in Room 17 (85); and four murex shell trumpets and the mouthpiece from a fifth in Room 38 (190).

9. The actual number in the American Museum of Natural History collection from Pueblo Bonito is H/10418.

10. Akins's Appendix B: Chaco Burial Data (1986, 162–63) includes data for the burials in Rooms 32 and 33. However, she does not include them in Appendix A: Biological Studies Data (143–45); nor are skeletons 13 and 14 listed among those in table A.4: Arthritis and Trauma (149). Furthermore, there is no discussion of any trauma to the two individuals in the text (117, 131–33). These omissions are curious.

11. See Pepper's notes (1905, 1909, and 1920) on Rooms 28, 28a, 32, 38, and 51–57, especially 53 and 56.

12. "Near" is a relative term. There were certainly some burial mounds just across the arroyo, to the west, as noted in Marietta Wetherill's (1948) account recorded by Gordon Vivian, and elsewhere, as discussed below and in Pepper's (1909) own comments on page 248.

13. But both skeleton 13 and skeleton 14 were murdered—hardly a "mark of respect"—and Pepper did not recognize them as murder victims.
14. As I noted earlier, the same is true for the number of hearths in both Judd's and Pepper's published reports.

CHAPTER FOUR

1. Wind and blowing sand can rapidly cover and uncover features at Chaco Canyon. In the winter of 1969, while conducting reconnaissance, I observed a gridded field on the first bench of the mesa above Chetro Ketl. The wind was blowing hard. When I returned the next day to photograph the feature, I found it so covered over by sand that it was no longer visible. I did not have the opportunity to photograph it until several years later and have noticed its appearance/disappearance over the course of a couple of decades of fieldwork at the canyon. The same thing occurred a few years later in the arroyo below Peñasco Blanco. Looking down from the north end of the site to the arroyo, I saw a fragment of a large stone wall extending from the south embankment of the arroyo. I planned to visit it the next day to photograph what I believed was part of an ancient dam or irrigation channel wall. That night there was a storm with high winds, and when I arrived at the area in mid-morning, the wall was covered with sand and nowhere to be seen.
2. It must be noted that Pepper's written description here is incorrect and presumably he did not make this error during the actual lecture. The large mound, Mound 5, was *not* at the foot of the talus and was much higher than two or three feet. It was out in the flat, as is clear in figure A.2, and could not have been formed by soil washing down from the mesa. The Wetherill burial site in the cemetery created by Marietta Wetherill (plates 6–7) west of Pueblo Bonito may be one of these ancient mounds at the foot of the talus. If so, it fits well with Pepper's description.
3. In fact, Wetherill dug in both these mounds before Pepper first set foot in Chaco Canyon in the spring of 1896: "A body was found in a narrow strip between two holes that had been dug by the Wetherill party during the winter of 1895–1896" (Pepper 1920, 341).

4. The Chaco Digital Initiative has a photograph of Mound 1, probably taken by Wetherill, with his brother-in-law and freighter, Orion Buck, standing atop it. It can be viewed at http://www.chacoarchive.org by typing the words "Burial Mound 1" without quotation marks into the Search All Fields box.
5. Two points must be made: First, this is not the same Mound 5 discussed by Pepper, for which we have photographs of some of the burials (figures A.1 and 3–8). Wetherill seems to have had his own numbering sequence, at least initially. Second, this makes it clear that Wetherill knew the difference between a burial mound and a house mound.
6. This could be one of the two small burial mounds shown in figure 19.
7. This again makes it clear that Wetherill could distinguish house mounds from burial mounds.
8. Unfortunately, the photographs are not numbered, nor does the notation on each one provide a number for the skeleton (the notations are not in either Pepper or Wetherill's handwriting). Therefore, we do not know whether these skeletons were uncovered toward the beginning of the excavation of Mound 5, later, or toward the cessation of the work. The only clue is that the skeletons appear to be fairly deep within the mound, which might suggest they were found some time after the excavation began.
9. While working at the Museum of the American Indian, Heye Foundation in the summers of 1980 and 1981, Nickels and I searched the attic where we were told the original Pepper–Wetherill negative plates were stored. It was hot, dirty work, but we located the plates and looked through them one by one. There were hundreds, but there were frequent gaps in the numbering; a large number were obviously missing. We asked museum staff about this, and they reported that a previous director had sold off the "duplicates" to raise money. Given how slow photography was at the time, photographing live action scenes did not produce duplicates. Rather, the plates were silver-coated, and the price of silver soared in the early 1970s when the Hunt brothers tried to corner the silver market. It's possible that some plates containing images of mounds and burials were sold in the process and destroyed for their silver content. We presume the remaining plates are now housed at the National Museum of the American Indian in Washington, DC.

APPENDIX B

1. Based on a reevaluation of tree-ring dates, Lekson (1984a) dates the Medio Period to AD 1150–1450, and Ravesloot et al. (1995) assign it a date of AD 1200–1500.

APPENDIX C

1. Pepper was associated with the American Museum of Natural History until 1909, so it is somewhat surprising that he did not ask one of the botanists there to identify it.
2. Pepper apparently never responded to her request, but the seeds were from Pueblo Bonito.

REFERENCES

Akins, Nancy J. 1986. *A Biocultural Approach to Human Burials from Chaco Canyon, New Mexico.* Reports of the Chaco Center 9. Santa Fe: National Park Service.

———. 2003. "The Burials of Pueblo Bonito." In *Pueblo Bonito, Center of the Chacoan World*, edited by Jill E. Neitzel, 94–106. Washington, DC: Smithsonian Books.

Akins, Nancy J., and John D. Schelberg. 1984. "Evidence for Organizational Complexity as Seen from Mortuary Practices at Chaco Canyon." In Judge and Schelberg, *Recent Research on Chaco Prehistory*, 89–102.

Bass, William M. 1971. *Human Osteology: A Laboratory and Field Manual of the Human Skeleton.* Columbia: Missouri Archaeological Society.

Bennett, Kenneth A. 1975. *Skeletal Remains from Mesa Verde National Park, Colorado.* Archaeological Research Series 7F. Washington, DC: National Park Service.

Bernardini, Wesley. 1999. "Reassessing the Scale of Social Action at Pueblo Bonito, Chaco Canyon, New Mexico." *Kiva* 64(4): 447–70.

Brand, Donald D., Florence M. Hawley, Frank C. Hibben, and Donovan Senter. 1937. *Tseh So, A Small House Ruin, Chaco Canyon, New Mexico: Preliminary Report.* University of New Mexico Bulletin, Anthropological Series 2(2). Albuquerque: University of New Mexico.

Brothwell, Don R. 1972. *Digging up Bones: The Excavation, Treatment, and Study of Human Skeletal Remains.* 2nd ed. London: British Museum (Natural History).

Brugge, David M. 1964. "Vizcarra's Navajo Campaign of 1823." *Arizona and the West* 6(3): 223–44.

Bryan, Kirk. 1954. *The Geology of Chaco Canyon, New Mexico in Relation to the Life and Remains of the Prehistoric Peoples of Chaco Canyon.* Smithsonian Miscellaneous Collections, Volume 122, Number 7. Washington, DC: Smithsonian Institution.

REFERENCES

Bunzel, Ruth. 1932. *Zuñi Origin Myths.* Bureau of American Ethnology Annual Report 47: 545–610. Washington, DC: Smithsonian Institution.

Butler, Barbara H. 1971. "The People of Casas Grandes: Cranial and Dental Morphology through Time." PhD dissertation, Southern Methodist University.

Coltrain, Joan Brenner, Joel C. Janetski, and Shawn W. Carlyle. 2007. "The Stable- and Radio-Isotope Chemistry of Western Basketmaker Burials: Implications for Early Puebloan Diets and Origins." *American Antiquity* 72(2): 301–21.

Corruccini, Robert S. 1972. "The Biological Relationships of Some Prehistoric and Historic Pueblo Populations." *American Antiquity* 44(3): 405–29.

Crown, Patricia L., ed. 2016. *The Pueblo Bonito Mounds of Chaco Canyon: Material Culture and Fauna.* Albuquerque: University of New Mexico Press.

———. 2020. *The House of the Cylinder Jars: Room 28 in Pueblo Bonito, Chaco Canyon.* Albuquerque: University of New Mexico Press.

Crown, Patricia L., and William Jeffrey Hurst. 2009. "Evidence of Cacao Use in the Prehispanic American Southwest." *Proceedings of the National Academy of Sciences* 106(7): 2110–13.

Crown, Patricia L., Kerriann Marden, and Hannah Mattson. 2016. "Foot Notes: The Social Implications of Polydactyly and Foot-Related Imagery at Pueblo Bonito, Chaco Canyon." *American Antiquity* 81(3): 426–48.

Cully, Anne C. 1985. "Appendix A. Checklist of Plants, Chaco Canyon, National Monument." In *Environment and Subsistence of Chaco Canyon*, edited by Frances Joan Mathien, 447–57. Publications in Archeology 18E, Chaco Canyon Studies. Albuquerque: National Park Service.

Curtis, Edward S., ed. 1926. *The North American Indian.* Vol. 17: *The Tewa. The Zuñi.* Norwood, MA: Plimpton Press.

Cushing, Frank Hamilton. 1896. *Outlines of Zuñi Creation Myths.* Bureau of American Ethnology Annual Report 13: 321–427. Washington, DC: Smithsonian Institution.

———. 1920. *Zuñi Breadstuff.* Indian Notes and Monographs 8. New York: Museum of the American Indian, Heye Foundation.

Dorsey, George A. 1904. Letter to the Wetherill Mercantile Company (Richard Wetherill), December 14. Field Museum of Natural History, Chicago, Illinois.

REFERENCES

Douglass, Andrew E. 1935. *Dating Pueblo Bonito and Other Ruins of the Southwest.* Contributed Technical Papers, Pueblo Bonito Series, 1. Washington, DC: National Geographic Society.

Durand, Kathy Roler. 2003. "Function of Chaco-Era Great Houses." *Kiva* 69(2): 141–69.

Dutton, Bertha P. 1938. *Łeyit Kin: A Small House Ruin, Chaco Canyon, New Mexico.* School of American Research Monograph 7. Albuquerque: University of New Mexico.

Elliott, Melinda. 1995. *Great Excavations: Tales of Early Southwestern Archaeology, 1889–1939.* Santa Fe: School of American Research.

El-Najjar, Mahmoud Y., and K. Richard McWilliams. 1978. *Forensic Anthropology.* Springfield, IL: Charles C. Thomas.

Espinosa, Nancy Sweet. 2006. "Human Remains from Salmon Pueblo, 2005. Update." In *Thirty-Five Years of Archaeological Research at Salmon Ruins, New Mexico.* Vol. 1: *Introduction, Architecture, Chronology, and Conclusions,* edited by Paul F. Reed, 331–48. Tucson: Center for Desert Archaeology/Bloomfield, NM: Salmon Ruins Museum.

Fewkes, J. Walter. 1920. "Sun Worship of the Hopi Indians." *Smithsonian Institution Annual Report for 1918*: 493–526.

Fricke, Mary Louise. 1979. "A Re-Investigation and Re-Evaluation of the Burial Rooms and Room 28 from Pueblo Bonito, Chaco Canyon, New Mexico." Unpublished typescript in possession of the author.

Genovés, Santiago (1967). "Proportionality of the Long Bones and Their Relation to Stature among Mesoamericans." *American Journal of Physical Anthropology* 26(1): 67–77.

Gilbert, B. Miles, and Thomas W. McKern. 1973. "A Method for Aging the Female Os Pubis." *American Journal of Physical Anthropology* 38(1): 31–38.

Gruner, Erina. 2017. "The Mobile House: Religious Leadership at Chacoan and Chacoan Revival Centers." In *Religion and Politics in the Ancient Americas,* edited by Sarah B. Barber and Arthur A. Joyce, 27–50. London: Routledge.

Hawley, Florence M. 1934. *Significance of the Dated Prehistory of Chetro Kettle, Chaco Cañon, New Mexico.* School of American Research Monograph 2. Albuquerque: University of New Mexico.

Hayes, Alden C., Jon Nathan Young, and A. H. Warren. 1981. *Excavation of Mound 7, Gran Quivira National Monument, New Mexico*. Publications in Archaeology 16. Washington, DC: National Park Service.

Hewett, Edgar L. 1921. "The Chaco Canyon and Its Ancient Monuments." *Art and Archaeology* 11(1–2): 3–28.

———. 1936a. *The Chaco Canyon and Its Monuments*. Handbooks of Archaeological History. Albuquerque: University of New Mexico and School of American Research.

———. 1936b. *The Pajarito Plateau and its Ancient Peoples*. Albuquerque: University of New Mexico Press.

Holsinger, S[amuel] J. 1901. Report on the Prehistoric Ruins of Chaco Canyon, New Mexico, Ordered by the General Land Office Letter "P," December 18, 1900. 3 vols. Washington, DC: National Anthropological Archives.

Hooten, Earnest A. 1930. *The Indians of Pecos Pueblo*. New Haven, CT: Yale University Press.

Hrdlička, Aleš. n.d. "Brief Report on the Skeletal Material from Pueblo Bonito and Nearby Ruins, New Mexico, Collected by Neil M. Judd." Archive 0028C, 2130C, 2211, National Park Service, Chaco Culture National Historical Park Museum Archive, University of New Mexico, Albuquerque.

———. 1931. "Catalog of Human Crania in the U.S. National Museum Collections." *U.S. National Museum Proceedings* 78(2845): 1–95.

Judd, Neil M. 1930. "The Excavation and Repair of Betatakin." *Proceedings of the United States National Museum* 77(5): 1–77. Washington, DC: Smithsonian Institution.

———. 1954. *The Material Culture of Pueblo Bonito*. Smithsonian Miscellaneous Collections, Volume 124. Washington, DC: Smithsonian Institution.

———. 1959. *Pueblo del Arroyo, Chaco Canyon, New Mexico*. Smithsonian Miscellaneous Collections, Volume 137, No. 1. Washington, DC: Smithsonian Institution.

———. 1964. *The Architecture of Pueblo Bonito*. Smithsonian Miscellaneous Collections, Volume 147, No. 1. Washington, DC: Smithsonian Institution.

Judge, W. James, and John D. Schelberg, eds. 1984. *Recent Research on Chaco Prehistory*. Reports of the Chaco Center 8. Albuquerque: National Park Service.

REFERENCES

Kennett, Douglas J., Steven Plog, Richard J. George, et al. 2017. "Archaeogenomic Evidence Reveals Prehistoric Matrilineal Dynasty." *Nature Communications* 8: 14115. https://doi.org/10.1038/ncomms14115.

Kidder, Alfred V. 1924. *An Introduction to the Study of Southwestern Archaeology with a Preliminary Account of the Excavations at Pecos*. New Haven, CT: Department of Archaeology, Phillips Academy, by Yale University Press.

———. 1958. *Pecos, New Mexico: Archaeological Notes*. Papers of the Robert S. Peabody Foundation for Archaeology 5. Andover, MA: Phillips Academy.

Kluckhohn, Clyde, and Paul Reiter, eds. 1939. *Preliminary Report on the 1937 Excavations, Bc 50–51, Chaco Canyon, New Mexico*. University of New Mexico Bulletin, Anthropological Series 3(2). Albuquerque: University of New Mexico.

Lange, Charles H. and Carroll L. Riley, eds. 1966. *The Southwestern Journals of Adolph F. Bandelier, 1880–1882*. Albuquerque: University of New Mexico Press.

Lekson, Stephen H. 1984a. "Dating Casas Grandes." *The Kiva* 50: 55–60.

———. 1984b. "Standing Architecture at Chaco Canyon and the Interpretation of Local and Regional Organization." In Judge and Schelberg, *Recent Research on Chaco Prehistory*, 55–73.

———. 1988. "The Idea of Kiva in Anasazi Archaeology." *Kiva* 53(3): 213–34.

Lister, Robert H., and Florence C. Lister. 1981. *Chaco Canyon Archaeology and Archaeologists*. Albuquerque: University of New Mexico Press.

Luhrs, Dorothy. 1935. "The Excavation of Kin Nahasbas, Chaco Cañon, New Mexico." Chaco Center Archives, University of New Mexico, Albuquerque.

Maher, Robert F. 1947. "A Report on Excavations in Search of a Burial Ground at Bc-48 (Archive 393)." Manuscript on file, National Park Service Branch of Cultural Research, Albuquerque.

Marden, Kerriann. 2011. "Taphonomy, Paleopathology and Mortuary Variability in Chaco Canyon: Using Bioarchaeological and Forensic Methods to Understand Ancient Cultural Practices." Unpublished PhD dissertation, Tulane University.

———. 2015. "Human Burials of Chaco Canyon: New Developments in

Cultural Interpretations through Skeletal Analysis." In *Chaco Revisited: New Research on the Prehistory of Chaco Canyon*, edited by Carrie C. Heitman and Stephen Plog, 162–86. Tucson: University of Arizona Press.

Mathien, Frances Joan, and Thomas C. Windes. 1987. *Kin Nahasbas Ruin, Chaco Culture National Historical Park, New Mexico*. Santa Fe: National Park Service.

McGregor, John C. 1943. "Burial of an Early American Magician." *Proceedings of the American Philosophical Society* 86(2): 270–95.

McKenna, Peter J., and Marcia L. Truell. 1986. *Small Site Architecture of Chaco Canyon, New Mexico*. Publications in Archeology 18D. Chaco Canyon Studies. Santa Fe: National Park Service.

McKern, Thomas W., and T. Dale Stewart. 1957. *Skeletal Age Changes in Young American Males: Analysed from the Standpoint of Age Identification*. Technical Report EP-45. Natick, MA: Headquarters, Quartermaster Research and Development Command.

McNitt, Frank. 1966. *Richard Wetherill: Anasazi*. Rev. ed. Albuquerque: University of New Mexico Press.

Miller, James M. 1937. "The G Kivas of Chettro Kettle." MA thesis, University of Southern California, Los Angeles.

Mills, Barbara J. 2018. "What's New in Chaco Research?" *Antiquity* 92(364): 855–69.

Mills, Barbara J., and T. J. Ferguson. 2008. "Animate Objects: Shell Trumpets and Regional Networks in the Greater Southwest." *Journal of Archaeological Method and Theory* 15(4): 338–61.

Mindeleff, Victor. 1891. *A Study of Pueblo Architecture: Tusayan and Cibola*. Bureau of American Ethnology, 8th Annual Report, 3–228. Washington, DC: Smithsonian Institution.

Moorehead, Warren K. 1906. *A Narrative of Explorations in New Mexico, Arizona, Indiana, Etc. Together with a Brief History of the Department*. Andover, MA: Phillips Academy.

Morris, Anne Axtell. 1934. *Digging in the Southwest*. Garden City, NY: Doubleday, Doran.

Nelson, Nels C. 1914. *Pueblo Ruins of the Galisteo Basin, New Mexico*. Anthropological Papers, Volume 15, Part 1. New York: American Museum of Natural History.

———. 1916. "Chronology of the Tano Ruins, New Mexico." *American Anthropologist* 18: 159–80.

Nickels, Martin K., and Jonathan E. Reyman. 1981. "New Analyses of Burial Rooms 32–33 at Pueblo Bonito: The Human Skeletal Remains." Presentation, 46th Annual Meeting of the Society for American Archaeology, San Diego.

Palkovich, Ann M. 1980. *Pueblo Population and Society: The Arroyo Hondo Skeletal and Mortuary Remains*. Santa Fe: School of American Research.

———. 1984. "Disease and Mortality Patterns in the Burial Rooms of Pueblo Bonito: Preliminary Considerations." In Judge and Schelberg, *Recent Research on Chaco Prehistory*, 103–14.

Parsons, Elsie Clews. 1932. "Isleta, New Mexico." *47th Annual Report of the Bureau of American Ethnology*, 193–466. Washington, DC: Smithsonian Institution.

———. 1939. *Pueblo Indian Religion*. Chicago: University of Chicago Press.

Pepper, George H. 1896a. Field Diary (May 4, 1896–November 13, 1896). Museum of the American Indian/Heye Foundation Records, Box 188, Smithsonian Institution, National Museum of the American Indian, Washington, DC.

———. 1896b. Pueblo Bonito Field Notes. Museum of the American Indian/Heye Foundation Records, Box 188, Smithsonian Institution, National Museum of the American Indian, Washington, DC.

———. 1897. Hyde Exploring Expedition Field Notes. Latin American Library, Tulane University, New Orleans.

———. 1899a. Chaco Canyon Field Notes. Museum of the American Indian/Heye Foundation Records, Box 188, Smithsonian Institution, National Museum of the American Indian, Washington, DC.

———. 1899b. Notes for a lecture at the American Museum of Natural History (March 18, 1899). American Museum of Natural History, New York.

———. 1903. Inventory, Hearst Southwestern Pottery Collection. Typescript. Museum of the American Indian/Heye Foundation Records, Box 188, Smithsonian Institution, National Museum of the American Indian, Washington, DC.

———. 1905. "Ceremonial Objects and Ornaments from Pueblo Bonito, New Mexico." *American Anthropologist* N.S. 7(2): 182–97.

———. 1909. "The Exploration of a Burial-Room in Pueblo Bonito, New Mexico."

In *Putnam Anniversary Volume: Anthropological Essays, Presented to Frederic Ward Putnam in Honor of His Seventieth Birthday, April 16, 1909, by His Friends and Associates*, 196–252. New York: G. P. Stechert.

———. 1920. *Pueblo Bonito*. Anthropological Papers, Volume 27. New York: American Museum of Natural History.

Plog, Stephen, and Carrie Heitman. 2006. "Understanding Chaco: A Digital Archival Approach." *Archaeology Southwest* 20(3): 17–18.

———. 2010. "Hierarchy and Social Inequality in the American Southwest, A.D. 800–1200." *Proceedings of the National Academy of Sciences of the United States of America* 107(46): 19619–26.

Plog, Stephen, and Peter M. Whiteley. 2018. "Dimensions and Dynamics of Pre-Hispanic Pueblo Organization and Authority: The Chaco Canyon Conundrum." In *Puebloan Societies: Cultural Homologies in Time and Space*, edited by Peter Whiteley, 237–60. Albuquerque: University of New Mexico Press.

Ravesloot, John C, Jeffrey S. Dean, and Michael S. Foster. 1995. "A New Perspective on the Casas Grandes Tree-Ring Dates." In *The Gran Chichimeca: Essays on the Archaeology and Ethnohistory of Northern Mesoamerica*, edited by Jonathan E. Reyman, 240–51. Worldwide Archaeology Series 12. Aldershot, Hampshire: Avebury Press.

Reid, Jefferson, and Stephanie Whittlesey. 1999. *Grasshopper Pueblo: A Story of Archaeology and Ancient Life*. Tucson: University of Arizona Press.

Reyman, Jonathan E. 1971. "Mexican Influence on Southwestern Ceremonialism." PhD dissertation, Southern Illinois University, Carbondale.

———. 1978a. "*Pochteca* Burials at Anasazi Sites?" In *Across the Chichimec Sea: Papers in Honor of J. Charles Kelley*, edited by Carroll L. Riley and Basil C. Hedrick, 242–59. Carbondale: Southern Illinois University Press.

———. 1978b. "Room 44, Wupatki: Rejecting False Profits." *American Antiquity* 43: 729–33.

———. 1982. Review of Williamson, Archaeoastronomy in the Americas. *American Antiquity* 47: 905–7.

———. 1985. "A Reevaluation of Bi-wall and Tri-wall Structures in the Anasazi Area." In *Contributions to the Archaeology and Ethnohistory of Greater Mesoamerica*, edited by W. J. Folan, 292–334. Carbondale. Southern Illinois University Press.

———. 1987. Review of Judge and Schelberg, *Recent Research on Chaco Prehistory*. *The Kiva* 52: 147–51.

———. 1989. "The History of Archaeology and the Archaeological History of Chaco Canyon, New Mexico." In *Tracing Archaeology's Past: The Historiography of Archaeology*, edited by Andrew L. Christenson, 41–53. Carbondale: Center for Archaeological Investigations, Southern Illinois University Press.

———. 1990. "Rediscovered PseudoCloisonné from Pueblo Bonito: Description and Comparisons." In *Clues to the Past: Papers in Honor of William M. Sundt*, edited by M. S. Duran and D. T. Kirkpatrick, 217–28. Albuquerque: Archaeological Society of New Mexico.

———. 1992. "Women in Archaeology: Some Historical Notes and Comments." In *Rediscovering Our Past: Essays on the History of American Archaeology*, edited by Jonathan E. Reyman, 69–80. Worldwide Archaeology Series 2. Aldershot, Hampshire: Avebury Press.

———. 1995a. "*Pala´tkwabi:* The Red Land of the South." In *The Gran Chichimeca: Essays on the Archaeology and Ethnohistory of Northern Mesoamerica*, edited by Jonathan E. Reyman, 320–35. Worldwide Archaeology Series 12. Aldershot, Hampshire: Avebury Press.

———. 1995b. "Value in Mesoamerican-Southwestern Trade." In *The Gran Chichimeca: Essays on the Archaeology and Ethnohistory of Northern Mesoamerica*, edited by Jonathan E. Reyman, 271–80. Worldwide Archaeology Series 12. Aldershot, Hampshire: Avebury Press.

———. 2008. "Feathers and Ceremonialism in the American Southwest, Past and Present." *Journal of the West* 47(3): 16–22.

———. 2024. "Millions of Gifts for the Gods: The Feather Distribution Project." Unpublished manuscript under review for publication.

Reyman, Jonathan E., and Martin K. Nickels. 1981. "New Analyses of Burial Rooms 32–33 at Pueblo Bonito: The Artifacts." Presentation, 46th Annual Meeting of the Society for American Archaeology, San Diego.

Riley, Carroll L. 1954. "A Skeletal Series from Chaco Canyon." *El Palacio* 61(5): 156–58.

Robbins, Wilfred W., John P. Harrington, and Barbara Freire-Marreco. 1916. *The Ethnobotany of the Tewa Indians*. Bureau of American Ethnology Bulletin 55. Washington, DC: US Government Printing Office.

Roberts, Frank H. H. Jr. 1927. "The Ceramic Sequence in Chaco Canyon and Its Relationship to the Cultures of the San Juan Basin." PhD dissertation, Harvard University.

———. 1991. *The Ceramic Sequence in Chaco Canyon and Its Relationship to the Cultures of the San Juan Basin*. New York: Garland.

Senter, Donovan. 1937a. "Burials from Mound 50 and Mound 51." In Brand et al., *Tseh So, A Small House Ruin*, 140–62.

———. 1937b. "Tree Rings, Valley Floor Deposition, and Erosion in Chaco Canyon, New Mexico." *American Antiquity* 37(1): 68–75.

Shipman, Jeff H. 2006. "A Brief Overview of Human Skeletal Remains from Salmon Ruins." In *Thirty-Five Years of Archaeological Research at Salmon Ruins, New Mexico. Volume 1: Introduction, Architecture, Chronology, and Conclusions*, edited by Paul F. Reed, 327–30. Tucson: Center for Desert Archaeology/Bloomfield, NM: Salmon Ruins Museum.

Simmons, Leo W., ed. 1942. *Sun Chief: The Autobiography of a Hopi Indian*. New Haven, CT: Yale University Press.

Simpson, James H. 1850. "Journal of a Military Reconnaissance from Santa Fe, New Mexico to the Navaho Country, Made with the Troops under Command of Lt. Col. John M. Washington in 1849." Report to the Secretary of War, 31st Congress, 1st Session, Senate Executive Document 64, 56–139. Washington, DC: Union Office.

Smith, Watson. 1952a. *Excavations in Big Hawk Valley, Wupatki National Monument, Arizona*. Bulletin 24. Flagstaff: Museum of Northern Arizona.

———. 1952b. *Kiva Mural Decorations at Awatovi and Kawaika-a, with a Survey of Other Wall Paintings in the Pueblo Southwest*. Papers of the Peabody Museum of American Archaeology and Ethnology 38. Cambridge, MA: Harvard University.

———. 1991. *When is a Kiva? and Other Questions about Southwestern Archaeology*. Edited by Raymond H. Thompson. Tucson: University of Arizona Press.

Snead, James E. 2001. *Ruins and Rivals: The Making of Southwest Archaeology*. Tucson: University of Arizona Press.

Starn, Orin. 2004. *Ishi's Brain: In Search of America's Last "Wild" Indian*. New York: W. W. Norton.

Stephen, Alexander M. 1936. *Hopi Journal*. Edited by Elsie Clews Parsons. New York: Columbia University Press.

REFERENCES

Stevenson, Matilda Coxe. 1909. Letter to George H. Pepper, 2 September. National Museum of the American Indian, Washington, DC.

Stewart, T. Dale. 1975. "Study of Human Skeletal Remains from Pueblo Ruins in Chaco Canyon, New Mexico, 1935." In P. H. Oehser, ed., *National Geographic Society Research Report, 1890–1954 Projects*, 293–97. Washington, DC: National Geographic Society.

———. 1979a. *Essentials of Forensic Anthropology*. Springfield, IL: Charles C. Thomas.

———. 1979b. Letter to Jonathan E. Reyman, 12 February. Author's collection.

Suchey, Judy M. 1979. "Problems in the Aging of Females Using the Os Pubis." *American Journal of Physical Anthropology* 51(3): 467–70.

Todd, Thomas W. 1920. "Age Changes in the Pubic Bone: I: The Male White Pubis." *American Journal of Physical Anthropology* 3(3): 285–334.

Toll, H. Wolcott and Peter J. McKenna. 1997. "Chaco Ceramics." In *Ceramics, Lithics, and Ornaments of Chaco Canyon: Analysis of Artifacts from the Chaco Project, 1971–1978. Volume I: Ceramics*, edited by Frances Joan Mathien, 17–530. Publications in Archeology 18G, Chaco Canyon Studies. Santa Fe: National Park Service.

Ubelaker, Douglas H. 1978. *Human Skeletal Remains: Excavation, Analysis, Interpretation*. Chicago: Aldine.

Vivian, Gordon. 1948. Memorandum for Superintendent McNeil, Chaco Canyon (Interview with Mrs. Richard Wetherill). Chaco Center Archive, 657. National Park Service, Albuquerque.

Vivian, Gordon, and Paul Reiter. 1960. *Great Kivas of Chaco Canyon and Their Relationships*. School of American Research Monograph 22. Santa Fe: Museum of New Mexico.

Vivian, R. Gwinn, Dulce N. Dodgem, and Gayle H. Hartman. 1978. *Wooden Ritual Artifacts from Chaco Canyon, New Mexico: The Chetro Ketl Collection*. Anthropological Papers of the University of Arizona 32. Tucson: University of Arizona Press.

Vivian, R. Gwinn, and Bruce Hilpert. 2002. *The Chaco Handbook: An Encyclopedic Guide*. Salt Lake City: University of Utah Press.

Wetherill, Richard A. 1894. "Snider's Well." *The Archaeologist* 2: 288–89.

———. 1896. Field Notes. Museum of the American Indian/Heye Foundation Records, Box 188, Smithsonian Institution, National Museum of the American Indian, Washington, DC.

———. 1904. Letter to George A. Dorsey, November 26. Chicago: Field Museum of Natural History.

———. 1905. Letter to George A. Dorsey, January 10. Chicago: Field Museum of Natural History.

Williamson, Ray A. 1981. "North America: A Multiplicity of Astronomies." In *Archaeoastronomy in the Americas*, edited by Ray A. Williamson, 61–80. Los Altos, CA: Ballena Press.

Windes, Tom. 1984. "A New Look at Population in Chaco Canyon." In Judge and Schelberg, *Recent Research on Chaco Prehistory*, 75–87.

———. 1987. *Investigations at the Pueblo Alto Complex, Chaco Canyon, New Mexico, 1975–1979*. 2 vols. Publications in Archeology 18F. Chaco Canyon Studies. Santa Fe: National Park Service.

———. 1993. "The 1991 and 1992 Room Test Excavations at Pueblo Bonito." Manuscript on file, National Park Service Chaco Culture National Historical Park Museum Archive, University of New Mexico, Albuquerque.

———. 1997. Review of *Pueblo Bonito* by George H. Pepper. *The Kiva* 63(1): 87–89.

Windes, Thomas C., and Dabney Ford. 1996. "The Chaco Wood Project: The Chronometric Reappraisal of Pueblo Bonito." *American Antiquity* 61(2): 295–310.

Windes, Thomas C., and H. Wolcott Toll. 1987. *Investigations of the Pueblo Alto Complex, Chaco Canyon*. Vol. 2, Part 2: *Architecture and Stratigraphy*. Publications in Archeology 18E, Chaco Canyon Series. Santa Fe: National Park Service.

Woods, Margaret. 1935. "Report on Talus Unit No. 1." Typescript on file, Chaco Center Archives, University of New Mexico, Albuquerque.

INDEX

age, specimens, 132–33
Akins, Nancy, 3, 20–21, 24–26, 29–30, 75, 82, 88, 90–91, 99–102, 111–12, 131
American Museum of Natural History, 1, 14, 16, 31, 53, 68
Ancient Burial Mounds, label, 24
Arroyo de San Carlos, 10. *See also* Chaco Canyon, New Mexico
Arroyo House, 108–9
Asclepias macrotis Torr. *See* milkweed, identification of
Aztec Ruin, 31

Bass, William M., 130, 132
Bc sites. *See* Hosta Butte Phase sites
Belzoni, Giovanni, 34
Bennett, Kennet A., 136
Bernardini, Wesley, 20, 29, 112, 114
Betatakin, site, 44
Big Bead Mesa (Keur), 20
Big Hawk Valley report, 44
Bird Wing Design, 11
Bone Diggers, 99
Bonito Phase houses, absence of burials associated with, 28
Brain, C. K., 4
Broom, Robert, 4
Brothwell, Don R., 130

Bryan, Kirk, 109
Buck, Orion, 7, 99
Bureau of American Ethnology, 10
burial mounds: appearances, 98; coverage of, 92–94; general account of, 94–99; large burial mounds, 105–9; method of procedure, 95–96; photographs of, 95; place of operations, 97–98, 101; pottery arrangement, 96; skeletal remains found in, 98–99, 101–2; small burial mounds, 103–5; soil of, 94–96; usual form of burial, 96–97
burials: Chaco Canyon and, 10–34; ethics, morality, and practices, 33–34;grave goods, 30, 55, 100, 106–7; grave goods, absence, lack, or paucity of, 11, 33, 50, 53, 55, 73, 76, 83, 91, 100–101, 104; historical background on, 21–30; introduction to research on, 1–9; statement on apparent lack of, 21–23; unpublished data on, 50–56

Cameron, Jeanette, 2, 6, 8
Casa Rinconada, 13, 24–25, 48, 97, 103–5, 107, 149
CDI. *See* Chaco Digital Initiative

INDEX

cemeteries: appearances, 98; coverage of, 92–94; general account of, 94–99; large burial mounds, 105–9; method of procedure, 95–96; photographs of, 95; place of operations, 97–98, 101;

cemeteries (*continued*)
pottery arrangement, 96; skeletal remains found in, 98–99, 101–2; small burial mounds, 103–5; soil of, 94–96; usual form of burial, 96–97ceramics, 53, 109–10; at burials, 30; lack of analysis of, 36

Chaco Canyon, New Mexico, 1; archaeological reconnaissance, 10–11; case for unpublished record, 31–33; excavating small cemetery at, 101–2; historical background on burials, 21–30; historical interest of, 10; questions regarding, 20–21; trenching, 27–28; unpublished data on, 12–20; unpublished record for, 35–91

"Chaco Canyon and Its Ancient Monuments, The" (Hewett), 13

Chaco Digital Initiative (CDI), 31

Chaqueños, mortuary practice of, 25

Chetro Ketl, site, 12, 13–15, 24–25, 27, 99, 102, 150, 153–54; artifact assemblage of, 35; Great Sanctuary at, 88; G Kivas of, 46; kivas, 43–44; population estimates for, 29; surface area, 92

Chetro Ketl Talus Unit No. 1, site, 12

Chis-chillin-Begay, 94

crania, collecting, 34

cranial facial metrics, 141
cranial measurements, 133–34

decomposition, 91
de Forest–Hyde Expedition, 16
dendrochronology, 11
diaries, 6, 13–14, 33, 63, 94, 110
Douglass, A. E., 11

"Early American Magician," burial, 76, 82
estufa, 24, 37–38, 42, 85, 105
ethics, 33–34

Feather Distribution Project, 48, 49
Feinberg, Harold S., 72
Field Museum of Natural History, 8, 14, 102
field notes, 2, 5–6, 13–14, 25, 31–33, 36–38, 40, 43, 50, 53, 55, 61, 69, 84, 86, 99, 105–6, 110, 114, 128–29
flagstone floor, Old Bonitans, 88–89

Gilbert, B. Miles, 130
Gould, Richard, 1
Grand Gulch, 55
grave-digging, 34
grave robbers, 91, 99
great house(s), 10, 12, 15, 28–30, 39, 47, 48, 85, 153
Great Kiva(s), 36, 47–48, 151
Great Sanctuary, 27, 35–36, 38, 88, 151; term, 47–48, 151n8

Half House, site, 108–9
Hastings, Homer, 8, 148

INDEX

Hayden, F. V., 10
Hayes, Alden, 24, 28
Hearst, Phoebe Apperson, 16
Hearst, William Randolph, 16
Hearst Southwestern Pottery, 16
hearths: general presence of, 21, 32, 38, 40–41, 49, 56, 85, 154; revision upward of population estimates based on, 112–15; unpublished data on, 39–42
Heitman, Carrie, 47, 68, 82
Hewett, Edgar, 13, 24, 30, 46; assessment of, 25–26
Heye, George G., 16
Heye Foundation, 1–2
historical background, burials, 21–30; absence of burials associated with Bonito Phase houses, 28–29; apparent lack of burials, 21–23; asking where burials are, 25–27; focus on architecture, 29–30; Judd extended statement, 21–23; labeling "large circular structure," 24; omission in discussion, 24; population estimates, 29; trenching canyon, 27–28
Holsinger, S. J., 24, 34
Hopi, 41–43, 48, 80
Hosta Butte Phase, sites, 12, 24, 28, 51, 85
households, Pueblo Bonito, 29
Hrdlička, Aleš, 4, 80, 112
Hungo Pavi, 25, 29
Hyde Exploring Expedition, 1–2, 5, 6, 53, 94; and aerial photographs, 106–7; archaeological reconnaissance conducted by, 10–11; and burial mounds and cemeteries, 99–100; end of, 24; hearths excavated by, 40; Pepper papers and objects, 16–20; and unpublished data, 32; unpublished data of, 12–20
Hyde, B. Talbot, 16
Hyde, Frederick E., Jr., 16

individuals 13 and 14, Room 33: circumstances of attack on, 75; commissioned drawings, 77–79; context of burials of, 75–76, 80; discrepancies in specific measurements, 80–82; "elite" matriline, 74; invested wood objects, 82–83; lack of thorough excavation, 83–85; materials found with, 72–73; puncture wounds, 73–75
individuals, number of, 130–32

Jackson, Willim Henry, 10
Judd, Neil M., 5, 30, 32, 35, 86, 89–90, 111, 150n6; curious omission in discussion, 24; statement by, 21–23

katsinam, 48, 76
Kelley, J. Charles, 151n8
Kern, Edward, 10
Kern, Richard, 10
Keur, Dorothy L., 2, 6, 8, 20
key omissions, *Pueblo Bonito* (Pepper): burials, 50–56; hearths, 39–42; kivas, 42–49; Rooms 32–33, 56–72
Kidder, Alfred V., 149n5

171

INDEX

Kin Bineola, site, 112
Kin Nahasbas, site, 12, 48
kivas, unpublished data on: definitions, 42–44; as factor in size of habitation units, 42; Hewett concept of kivas, 46; lack of *sipapus*, 44–45; provocative essay on kivas, 45–49; residential and ceremonial structures, 49; terminology, 42; tower kivas, 43–44
Kroeber, A. L., 16

large burial mounds, excavating, 105–9
large circular structure. *See* Casa Rinconada
Latin American Library, Tulane University, 6–7, 15
Lekson, Stephen, 29, 45–49
Loew, Oscar, 10

Malot, Paul, 1
Marden, Kerriann, 3, 21, 80
masonry architecture, 37, 47, 48, 101
Mathien, Frances Joan, 31
Maxwell Museum of Anthropology, 2, 14
McKenna, Peter J., 36, 100–101
McKern, Thomas W., 130, 133, 139
McWilliams, Richard, 130
Mesa Verde, 43, 49, 55, 140–41, 150n5
Mesoamerican, 2, 5, 70, 86, 111, 153
Mesoamerican–Southwestern, 1
Middle American Research Institute, 2, 6, 15, 31
milkweed, identification of, 143–45

Mindeleff, Victor, 43
Moorehead, Warren K., 21, 38, 83, 101–2; ethics, morality, and practices of, 33–34
morality, 33–34
Morris, Anne Axtell, 43
Morrison, C. Randall "Randy," 14 149n2
Mound 1, 99–100, 103–5, 107, 155n4
Mound 2, 11, 53, 55, 103, 105, 107, 152n4
Mound 5, 6, 30, 34, 50–52, 93, 105–8, 111, 155n8; skeletal remains from, 117–25
Mound 7, 150n5
Mound 8, 105
Museum of the American Indian, 1–2, 5
Museum of the American Indian, Heye Foundation, 14–15

National Anthropological Archives, 14
National Geographic Society, 11, 35, 89
National Park Service Ruins Stabilization Unit, 13
National Science Foundation, 1
Native American Graves Protection and Repatriation Act, 34, 83
negative data, 40
Nelson, Nels, 33, 69
Nickels, Martin K., 2–5, 8, 63–64

"Ohmygod site," mystery of, 20
Old Bonitans, burial rooms, 86–87

painted altar cloth, 2–3, 111, 113

INDEX

Painted Stone Mortar, Room 80, 86–89
Palkovich, Ann M., 89, 91, 112
pathologies, 134–35
Peabody Museum, 5, 8, 14
Pecos Conference, 43
Peñasco Blanco, site, 86
Pennsylvania State University, 15
Pepper, George H., 1, 7, 11, 30, 32, 36, 92; considering papers and objects of, 16–20; ethics, morality, and practices of, 33–34; general account of burial mounds and cemeteries, 94–99; on large burial mounds, 103–5; on small burial mounds, 103–5
Pepper, Gertrude, 20
Pepper, Jeanette, 20
Pepper, Jessie Crellin, 6
perimortem trauma, evidence of, 73–74
Philadelphia Museum of Art, 15
Phoebe A. Hearst Museum of Anthropology, 16
photographs, aerial, 5, 14–15, 52, 106
pit house(s), 46–47
Plog, Stephen, 48, 68, 82, 91
population size/density, Chaco Canyon, 20–21, 39, 40
pottery, arrangement of, 96
Powell, Major J. W., 10
practices, 33–34
premortem trauma, evidence of, 73–74
primary data, sources of, 12–13, 32, 38, 89, 111, 114
pubic symphyseal age assessments, 139

Pueblo Alto, site, 14, 35, 98
Pueblo Bonito, site, 1, 11; aerial photograph of, 15; apparent lack of cemetery at, 21–23; burial mounds and cemeteries, 92–109; large burial mounds, 105–9; small burial mounds, 103–5; summaries of, 110–15; unpublished record for, 35–91
Pueblo Bonito (Pepper): burials, 50–56; Conclusion section, 92, 99; Foreword to, 36–37; hearths, 39–42; individuals 13 and 14, Room 33, 72–91; key omissions from, 39–72; kivas, 42–49; on large burial mounds, 105–9; Room 75 account, 37–38; Rooms 32–33, 56–72; small burial mounds, 103–5; summary and conclusions, 110–15
Pueblo del Arroyo, site, 11, 22, 24, 35, 50–52, 98, 102, 105; images from, 117–25
Pueblo Pintado, site, 50, 92, 106, 112, 114
Putnam, Frederick Ward, 11, 34
Putnam Anniversary Volume, 69, 72

Quetzalcoatl, 76

Reading Room, Latin American Library, 6–7
record, unpublished. *See* unpublished data
residential suites, Pueblo Bonito, 29
Roberts, Frank H. H., 32
Roberts, Frank H. H., Jr., 35

INDEX

Robert S. Peabody Institute of Archaeology, 8
Rodriguez, Anibal, 3
Room 13, Pueblo Bonito, 2, 111
Room 28, Pueblo Bonito, 3, 5, 61–62, 66, 69
Room 38, Pueblo Bonito, 3, 153n8
Room 53, Pueblo Bonito, 83–84
Room 61, Pueblo Bonito, 84, 86
Room 75, Pueblo Bonito, 37–38
Room 79, Pueblo Bonito, 85
Room 80, Pueblo Bonito, 85–86
Room 92, Pueblo Bonito, 42
Room 93, Pueblo Bonito, 13
Room 190, Pueblo Bonito, 11
Rooms 32–33, Pueblo Bonito, 4–5, 93, 104; commissioned drawings, 77–79; comparisons to other series, 135–36; contents in, 56; cranial measurements, 133–34; cylindrical vessels in, 69–70; deposition period, 82–83; discrepancies in specific measurements, 80–82; discussion of entry, 61–62; drawing of and notes on the stratigraphy in, 54; excavation and disposition, 127–29; field drawings, 57–61; foreign objects found in, 70–72; invested wood objects in, 82–83; methods of skeletal analysis, 129–30; number of individuals, 130–32; osteometric data and analysis, 127–41; pathologies, 134–35; physical conditions in, 64–68; sex and age of specimens, 132–33; skeletal remains found in, 62–64; Skeletons 13, 14, 15, 55; stature reconstruction, 134; stratigraphy of, 67–69; summary of, 137–41
Rooms 116–190, Pueblo Bonito, 11
Ruin Stabilization Reports, 12–13

Schelberg, John D., 111
Sellers, D. K. B., 111
Senter, Donovan, 26, 30
sepulture, 90
sex, specimens, 132–33
Simpson, James H., 10
sipapu, 44–45
skeletal analysis, methods of, 129–30
skeletal remains: comparisons to other series, 135–36; cranial measurements, 133–134; excavation and disposition, 127–29; methods of skeletal analysis, 129–30; number of individuals, 130–32; pathologies, 134–35; from Pueblo Bonito, 117–25; Room 80, 85; Rooms 32–33 (Pueblo Bonito), 62–64; Rooms 53, 61, 79, 83–85; sex and age of specimens, 132–33; stature reconstruction, 134; summary of, 137–41
skulls, measuring, 138
small burial mounds, excavating, 103–5
Smith, Watson, 44
Smithsonian Institution, 14
Snider, Julianne, 69
South Gap, Chaco Canyon, 100, 112
Southwest Cultural Resource Center, 5, 52–53, 106–7

specimens, sex and age of, 132–33
statue, reconstructing, 134
Stevenson, Matilda Coxe, 44, 143–44
Stewart, Potter, 43, 130
Stewart, T. Dale, 3
Strover, William, 24, 102

Talus Unit No. 1, site, 12
Teotihuacán Mapping Project, 31
Todd, Thomas W., 130, 133
Toll, H. Wolcott, 36
trait frequencies, 140
trenches, Mound 1, 99–100
trenching, Chaco Canyon, 27–28
Truell, Marica L., 100–101

Ubelaker, Douglas H., 130
Una Vida, site, 48
University of California Berkeley, 16
University of Pennsylvania, 15
unpublished data: additional architectural details, 37; burials, 50–56; case for, 31–33; difference between Pueblo Bonito and Chaco Canyon in terms of, 35; hearths, 39–42; individuals 13 and 14, Room 33, 72–91; key omissions, 39–72; kivas, 42–49; problem of unpublished data, 31–32; Pueblo Bonito Rooms 32–33, 56–72; Rooms 53, 61, 79, 83–85; Ruin Stabilization Reports, 12; sources of, 32–33; statement by Wissler, 36–37; summary of, 110–15; volumes on Pueblo Bonito, 35–36
US Geological and Geographical Survey, 10
US Land Office, 24

Vivian, Gordon, 14, 52, 92–93
Vivian, R. Gwinn, 13, 35
Vizcarra, José Antonio, 10

Wetherill, Marietta, 14, 52, 92–95, 150
Wetherill, Richard, 1, 7, 11, 13–14, 16, 31–32, 36, 50, 52, 92, 94–95, 99–100, 111, 150; ethics, morality, and practices of, 33–34
"When is a Kiva?" (Smith), 44–45
Wijiji, site, 47
Windes, Tom, 20, 21, 24, 29, 39, 40–41, 42, 45, 49, 112
Wupatki, 13, 148
Wissler, Clark, 36–38

Xipe Totec, 80

Zuñi, 23, 41, 80, 90, 114, 143, 145, 151

www.ingramcontent.com/pod-product-compliance
Lightning Source LLC
Chambersburg PA
CBHW052120300426
44116CB00010B/1741